Popular Teaching Resources

Art Lessons

Grades 5-6

Roland Giardetti • Monica Whatley

Printed in China

Contents

Guidelines for Use

This resource book contains three sections:

- Core Units
- Checklists
- Project Ideas

Each **Core Unit** is made up of an information sheet, two follow-up worksheets, and an activity for the entire class to do together. You will see that in all of the units, "Name", "Date", and the unit topic appear in each follow-up worksheet so that each one can stand on its own. There is more than one way to present each unit in the book. Here are two that may work for you: (1) give your students the lesson and the worksheets at the same time and let them work on both simultaneously, followed by the class activity; (2) give just the lesson and class activity one day and ask your students to underline key words and ideas or take notes as you talk about the subject, and then give them a worksheet the next day as a quiz.

The **Checklists** allow both you and your students to mark the students' progress and recognize which areas may need more study or attention.

The **Project Ideas** give students the opportunity to work creatively on projects that will help them develop their understanding of the material in many of the Core Units.

Happy teaching!

Art Lessons Grades 5-6

Music

Name: Date:

Reading Music

Objective: *To interpret correctly whole notes, half-notes, quarter-notes, eighth-notes, and the corresponding rests in 4/4 time*

How can musicians all over the world learn the same song, having never heard it before? Music has both sounds and silences that can be recorded on paper as notes and rests.

Learning to read music is like learning to read words. When you know how to do it, it opens up a whole new world. We can take a written piece and bring it to life!

Let's review the basics. We divide notes and rests into measures. Some notes and rests take up more "room" than others.

A staff with 4/4 time means the quarter note gets the beat and that there are 4 beats per measure.

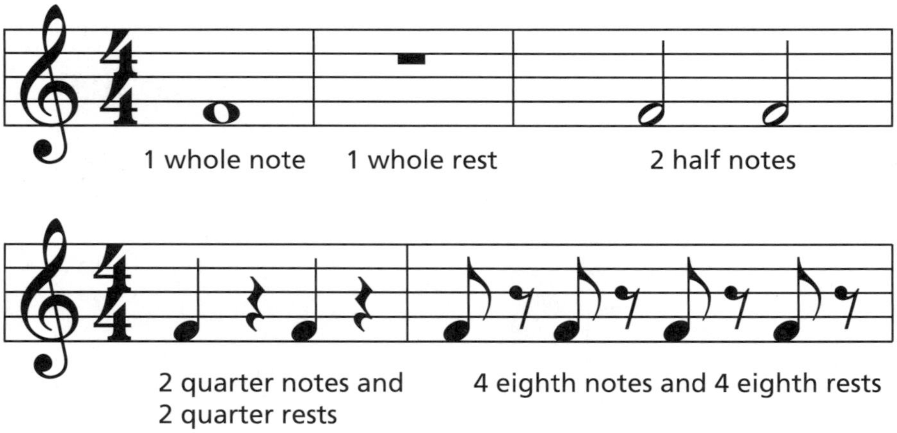

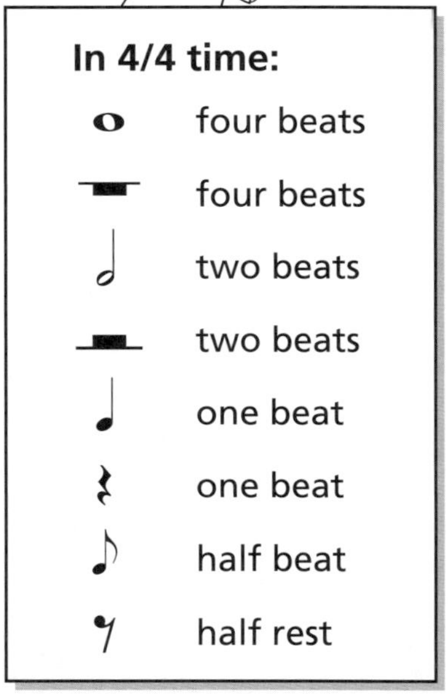

We can easily remember names of the notes on the lines of the staff with the saying, "**E**very **G**ood **B**oy **D**oes **F**ine." The spaces between these lines on the treble clef spell the word **F A C E**.

EGBDF (on the lines)

When we know what each note is (the pitch) and how long we make or hold the sound or rest for (duration), we can start singing or playing all kinds of music! We can write our own music to share with others, too!

FACE (between the lines)

Name: Date:

Reading Music

Quick Reference

EGBDF – the lines
FACE – the spaces

- 𝅝 whole note
- 𝄻 whole rest
- 𝅗𝅥 half note
- 𝄼 half rest
- ♩ quarter note
- 𝄽 quarter rest
- ♪ eighth note
- 𝄾 eighth rest

A. Identify and name the notes.

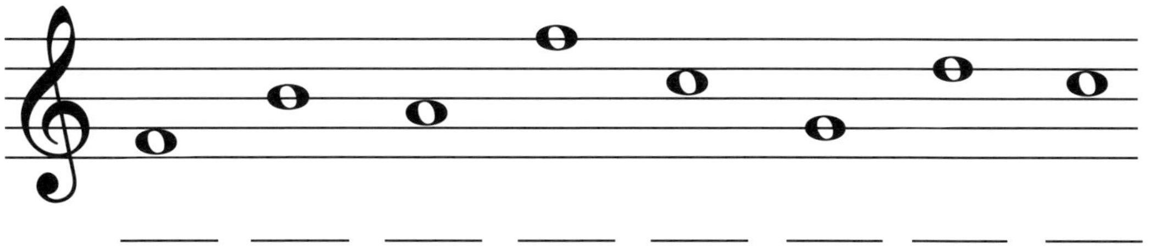

B. Record the notes on the staff for each set. The first one in each set is done for you.

1. beat ♩ ♩ ♩ ♩
   note E A D F

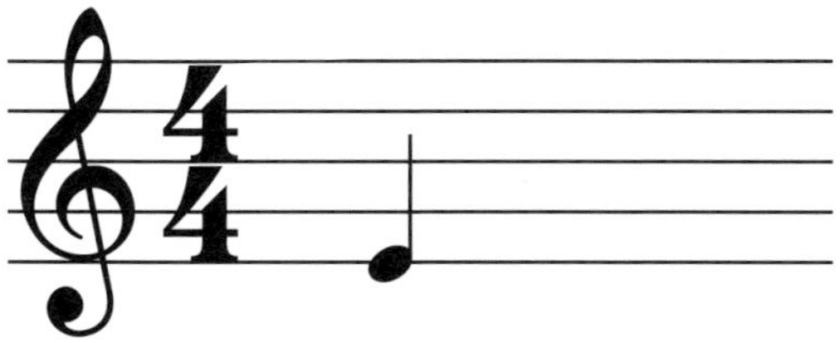

2. beat ♩ ♩ ♩ ♩
   note G C B A

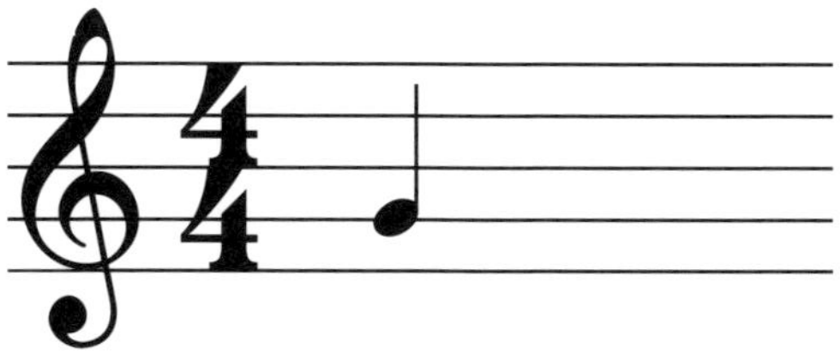

3. beat ♩ ♪ ♪ ♩ ♪ ♪
   note B F A D C B

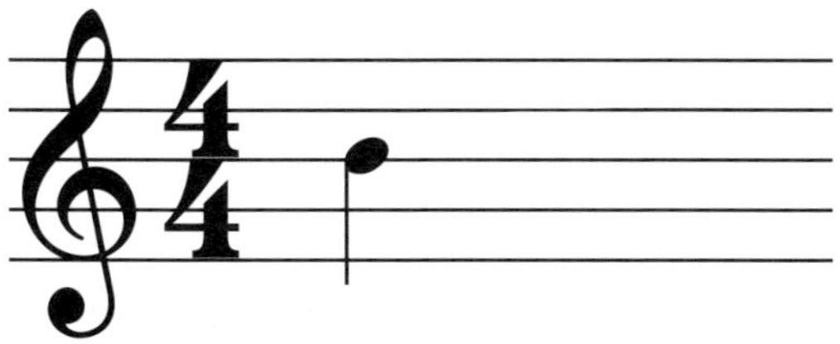

4. beat 𝅗𝅥 ♪ ♩ ♪ ♩ ♪ 𝅗𝅥 ♪
   note C A D F B G B C

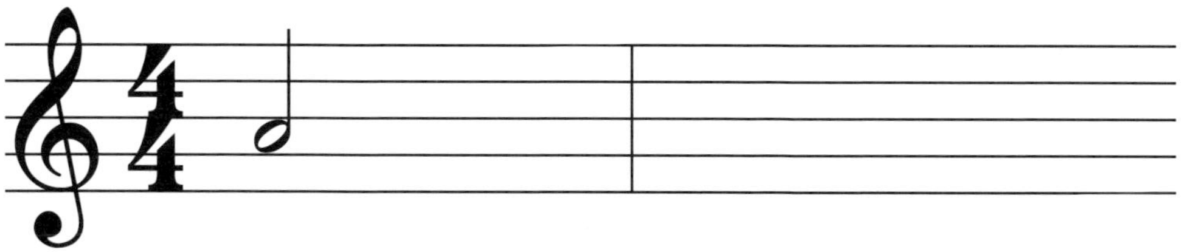

Name: Date:

Reading Music

Cut and paste the activity you want to do for each staff. Then do the activity with the class.

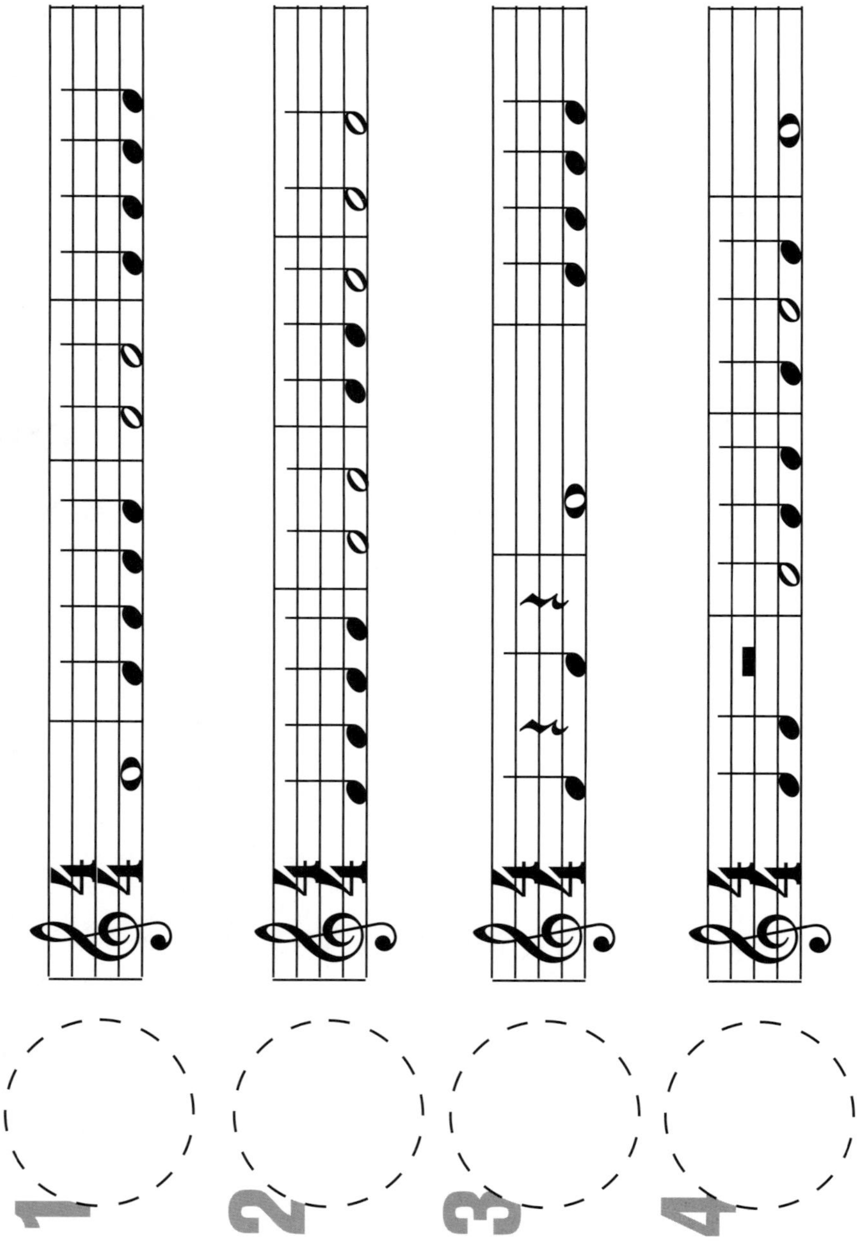

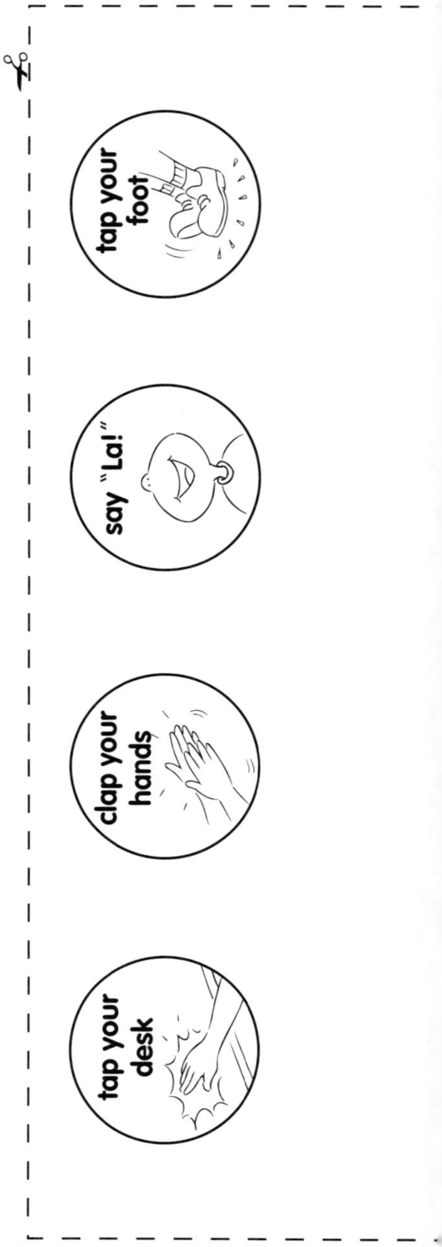

Name: Date:

Reading Music

Candy Music

Motivation:

To review note values and record notes

Materials:

- long pieces of shoe string licorice (six per student)
- Oreos – minis
- toothpicks
- tape
- cutouts of the treble clef, 4/4 (time), and rest shapes

What to Do:

1 Hand out five pieces of licorice per student. Have the students carefully stretch each piece horizontally across their desks to make a staff (each space wide enough to fit an Oreo). Tape the ends securely to the desk.

2 Cut the last piece to create bars, spaced evenly down the middle of the staff.

3 Use the cutouts to label treble clef and time signature.

4 Review the note values and show how each can be created with the Oreos and toothpicks:

- whole note – an opened, white Oreo
- half note – same as a whole note but with a toothpick as its stem
- quarter note – regular, black Oreo with a toothpick as its stem
- rest – the cut outs

5 Have students practise filling the two measures with notes in 4/4 time. They could make various combinations, including one whole note / one half note / one quarter note / one quarter rest, etc.

6 Review the tricks to remember the notes' names. Call out "A", "G", etc. and see if they know where to place their Oreos on the staff.

7 Have the students eat (the edible part of) their music!

Name: Date:

Sharps, Flats, and Naturals

Objective: *To demonstrate an understanding of the terms sharp, flat, and natural, and explain the use of key signatures*

What makes a song sound sad?

It could be the words, the instruments, or the way the music is played. Musicians can lower the pitch or sound of a note, making it flat and sad sounding.

Musicians can get a different sound by raising or lowering the pitch a little. A **sharp** sign means the note is one half step *higher* than the natural note. A **flat** sign means the note is one half step *lower* than the natural note.

If there is a sharp or flat, and the next note should be back the half step, then a **natural** symbol will be used for that measure.

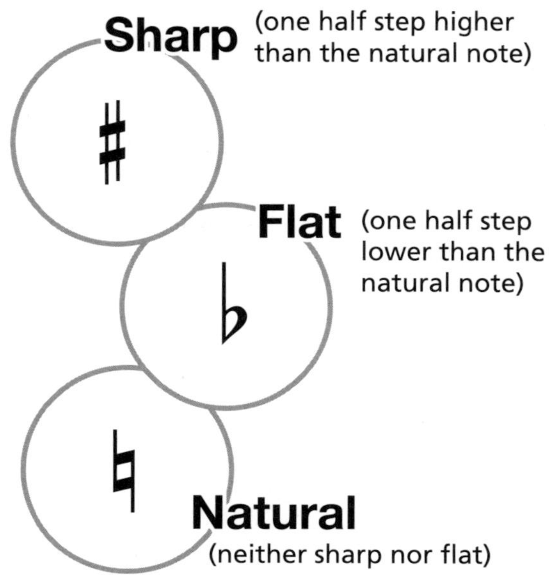

The **key signature** is a list of all the sharps and flats in the key that the music is in. When there is a sharp or flat on a line or space in the key signature, all the notes on that line or space will be sharp or flat.

If something is played or sung in the key of C major, there are no sharps or flats. This is probably the first scale a new musician will learn.

Name: Date:

Sharps, Flats, and Naturals

A. Copy each sign three times.

Sharp ♯	Flat ♭	Natural ♮

B. Circle the correct notes.

1. 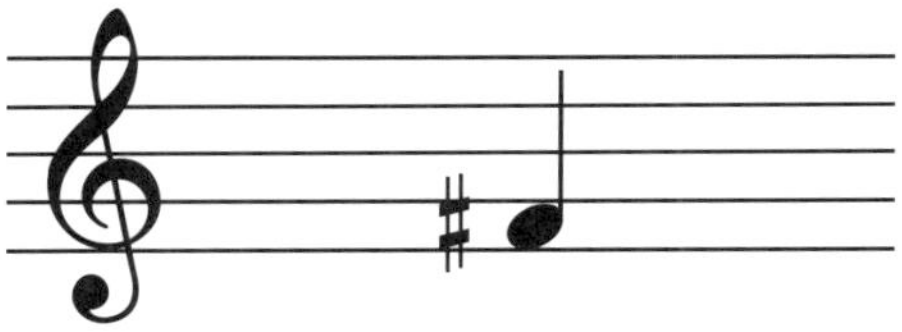

F sharp / F flat

2. 

B sharp / B natural

3. 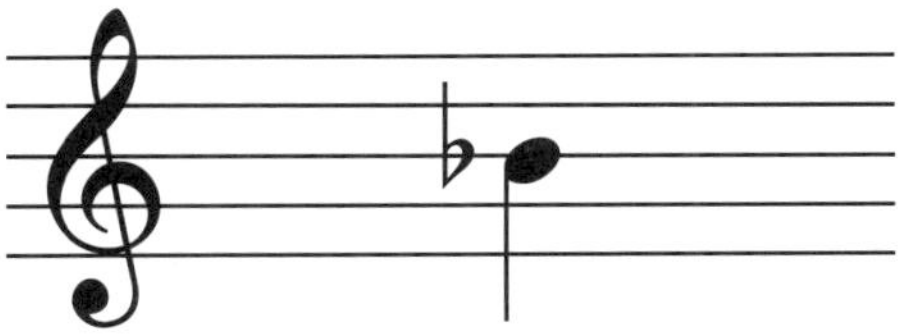

B natural / B flat

4. 

D sharp / D natural

5. 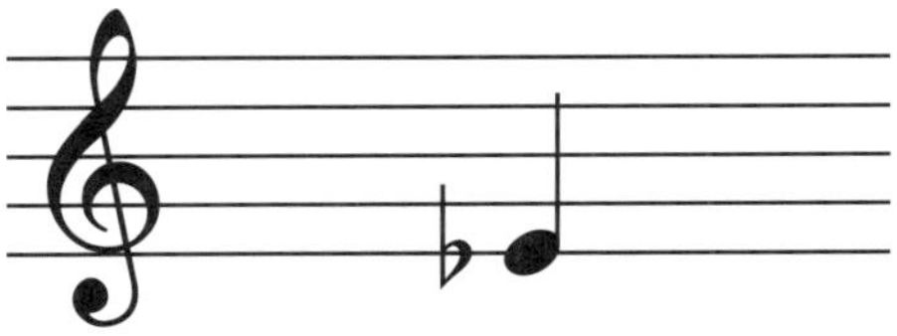

E flat / E sharp

6. 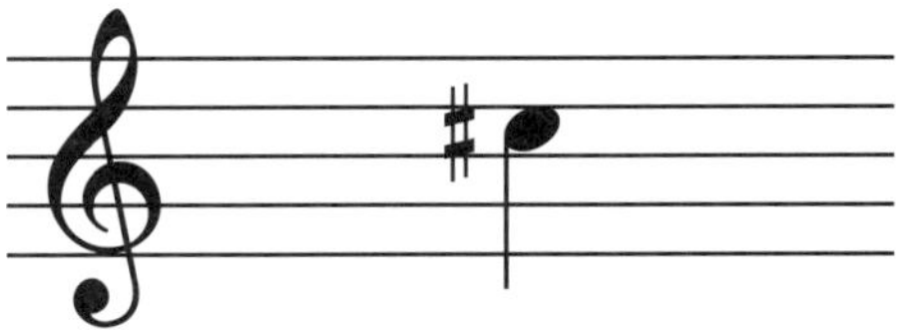

C sharp / C natural

7. 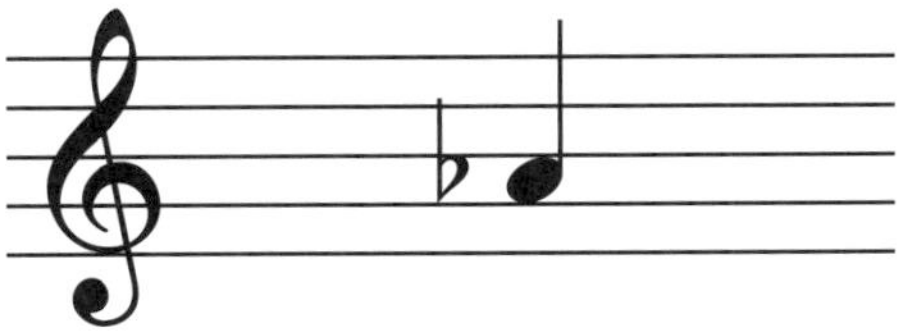

A flat / A sharp

8.  

D sharp / D natural

Name: Date:

Sharps, Flats, and Naturals

A. Cut and paste the correct notes.

1. 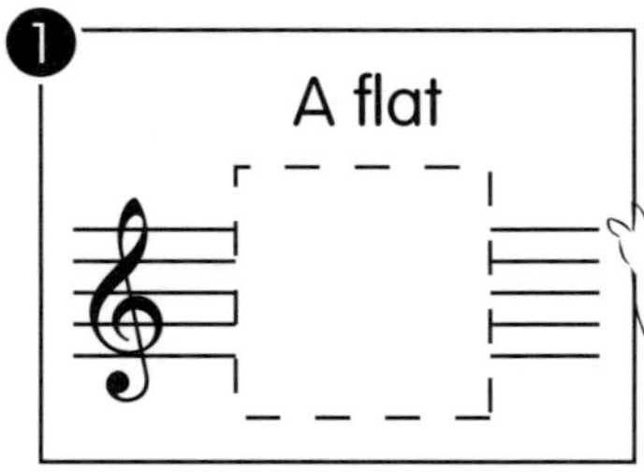

2. 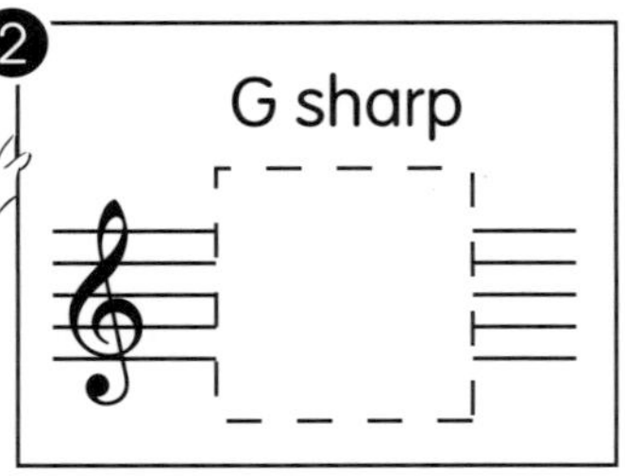

3. 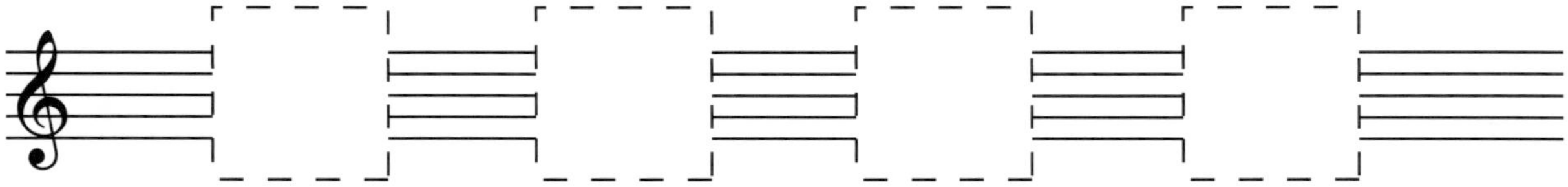

B. Write the notes.

G sharp **E flat** **A natural**

C natural **F sharp** **B flat**

Name: Date:

Sharps, Flats, and Naturals

Pop Bottle Pitches

Materials:

- glass bottle
- bowl
- pitcher of water
- funnel
- permanant marker
- instrument (i.e. piano, recorder) or tuning fork

Motivation:

To experiment with raising and lowering the pitch by a half step or a step

What to Do:

1 Use the funnel to pour enough water into the bottle so that it is a couple of centimetres high.

2 Blow across the opening of the bottle to make a note. On an instrument or tuning fork, play "C".

- Is your note lower or higher than this note?
- Does your note sound flat, sharp, or a half-step off?

Try to make the note natural by adding a little more water for a higher pitch or carefully pouring a little out into a bowl to make it lower.

3 Get into groups of four and place your bottles on a table in a row. Each bottle needs a different amount of water to make a different note. Use the funnel to add a little more water to the second, third, and fourth bottles. Again, try to adjust its pitch by adding more or less water, using the note on the instrument as a guide.

4 Label the notes on the bottles with permanent marker. ("C", "D", etc.)

Variation:

You can use your bottles as percussion instruments, too! Hit them with a wooden spoon and notice how the pitch changes!

Name: Date:

Introduction, Verse, and Chorus

Objective: *To identify the form of introduction, verse, and chorus and simple structural patterns in music that you sing, play, or hear*

What is the first song that comes to your mind? Is it one you sing every day, like O Canada, or was it the number one hit on the radio? Perhaps, it is a song you heard as a child, like *Old MacDonald.*

Many of the songs we sing are structured, making them fun to sing along to. They are usually divided into **verse-chorus form**. A song's **introduction** comes at the beginning of the piece and usually builds up a little suspense for the listener.

In music, the **chorus** is very different from the verse in its rhythm, melody (tune), and dynamics (volume). It is the part of a song that is highlighted and repeated over and over again. You would probably want to sing it a little louder, because you know it so well, and because it makes the music more interesting. For example:

"Let it be, let it be, let it be, let it be. Whisper words of wisdom, let it be."
(*Let It Be*, The Beatles, 1970)

The verse is usually what tells the story or idea of the song. It is like a poem and sometimes has a rhyming pattern. For example:

"There was a farmer had a dog, and Bingo was his name – Oh!"

Chorus and verse can be mixed with other types of patterns. AABA is a pattern in music often used in both jazz and popular music. The "A" parts are similar, while the "B" part (the bridge) is an entirely different section and prepares us to return to the "A".

Name: Date:

Introduction, Verse, and Chorus

Sing the song together. Identify the verse and chorus of the song. Write "V" for verse and "C" for chorus in the circles. Then complete the sentences.

My Bonnie Lies over the Ocean

◯ My Bonnie lies over the ocean
My Bonnie lies over the sea
My Bonnie lies over the ocean
Oh bring back my Bonnie to me

◯ Bring back, bring back
Bring back my Bonnie to me, to me
Bring back, bring back
Bring back my Bonnie to me

◯ Last night as I lay on my pillow
Last night as I lay on my bed
Last night as I lay on my pillow
I dreamed that my Bonnie was dead

◯ Bring back, bring back
Bring back my Bonnie to me, to me
Bring back, bring back
Bring back my Bonnie to me

◯ Oh blow ye the winds o'er the ocean
And blow ye the winds o'er the sea
Oh blow ye the winds o'er the ocean
And bring back my Bonnie to me

◯ Bring back, bring back
Bring back my Bonnie to me, to me
Bring back, bring back
Bring back my Bonnie to me

◯ The winds have blown over the ocean
The winds have blown over the sea
The winds have blown over the ocean
And brought back my Bonnie to me

◯ Bring back, bring back
Bring back my Bonnie to me, to me
Bring back, bring back
Bring back my Bonnie to me

1. There are ________ verses in the song.
2. The lyrics of the chorus are ____________________ .
   the same / different
3. The chorus and verse are mixed in the ____________________ pattern.
   ABABABAB / ABBAABBA

Name: Date:

Introduction, Verse, and Chorus

Write or paste a copy of the lyrics to your favourite song in the space below. Circle the verse with a blue crayon and the chorus with a red one. Then answer the questions.

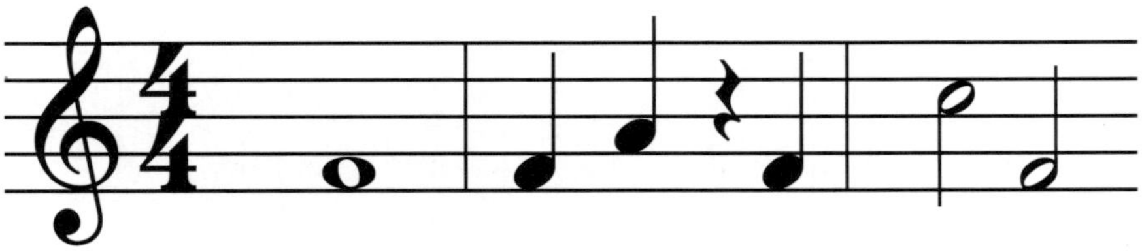

My Favourite Song

What is the pattern of the verses and chorus of this song? ______________

- Are the rhythm of the verse and the chorus the same? ______________
- Are the melody of the verse and the chorus the same? ______________

Name: Date:

Introduction, Verse, and Chorus

Singing Out

Materials:

- lyrics and recordings (see below)

Motivation:

To sing in tune (e.g. unison songs, "partner" songs, rounds) using suitable dynamics, tempo, and phrasing and manipulate a musical element to change the overall effect

Songs:

- Unison: *Yesterday* (The Beatles), *Yellow Submarine* (The Beatles)
- Round: *Oh How Lovely is the Evening*
- Partner songs: *She'll be Coming Round the Mountain/Wear a Smile* (Ruth E. Schram) or *Skip to My Lou/ Rock-a-my Soul*

What to Do:

1 Hand out the song sheets for *Yesterday* and ask someone to point out the difference between "verse" and "chorus" in *Yesterday*. Can you see the AABA pattern in the music?

2 Unison: Sing *Yesterday* and *Yellow Submarine*. Discuss how these two songs by the Beatles are different in tempo (speed), dynamics (volume), and phrasing. Change the speed, volume, and expression to alter the effect of the song.

- Can you make *Yesterday* sound cheerful or full of excitement?
- How many different ways can you sing the chorus of *Yellow Submarine*?

3 Introduce the idea that songs can be sung together, in partners or rounds.

4 Round: Split the class in thirds and practise *Oh How Lovely is the Evening* in a round.

5 Partner Songs: Split the class in half and have each side sing one of the partner songs.

Name: Date:

Music's Mood

Objective: *To recognize different kinds of tone colour in pieces of music and describe how the various elements of music are used to create mood in two pieces of music of different styles*

We love how music makes us feel and how it expresses what our own words can't say. Music can make us feel energetic or alive, melt a hard heart, or stir up anger. It can even bring on a feeling of fatigue and lull one to sleep. The mood that is created in a piece of music can have the effect of sweeping away its listeners.

The specific sound of an individual instrument or voice is its **tone colour**. What does this really mean? When you listen to music, is it whiny, breathy, raspy, metallic, buzzing, muted, brassy, reedy, brittle, wavering, light, clear, muddy, piercing, harsh...?

These are all adjectives describing tone colour and each has a mood attached to it. The metallic twang of the guitar will not put a baby to sleep. At a birthday party, a breathy, muted song may have guests wanting to sleep!

Listen to these songs and see what feelings or mood are created with the different tone colours, tempo (speed), dynamics (volume), and rhythm:

- *Great Balls of Fire* by Jerry Lee Lewis
- *Moonlight Sonata* by Beethoven
- *A Hard Day's Night* by The Beatles
- *I'm So Lonesome I Could Cry* by Hank Williams
- *The Entertainer* by Scott Joplin
- *Dance of the Sugar Plum Fairies* by Tchaikovsky

What adjectives would you use to describe the tone colour of these pieces?

Name: Date:

Music's Mood

Check the appropriate use of tone colour(s) in the music for each event.

1.

Tone Colour

- ◯ dull
- ◯ light
- ◯ metallic
- ◯ muted

2.

Tone Colour

- ◯ heavy
- ◯ light
- ◯ harsh
- ◯ buzzing

3.

Tone Colour

- ◯ wavering
- ◯ brassy
- ◯ breathy
- ◯ tickly

4.

Tone Colour

- ◯ buzzing
- ◯ breathy
- ◯ raspy
- ◯ clear

Name: Date:

Music's Mood

Name your favourite song. Check the appropriate terms that describe it. Then write the reasons why you like the song in the journal.

My Favourite Song

Tempo ○ slow ○ moderate ○ fast

Dynamics ○ soft ○ medium ○ loud

My Journal

- Why do you like the song?
- How does it make you feel when you listen to it?
- What specific sounds of the instruments or voices make it special?

Music's Mood

How Music Moves Us

Materials:

- theme song
- brush
- water
- heavy paper (9 x 12")
- pencil
- Styrofoam tray
- rag and/or sponge – optional
- watercolour paint (a variety of colours)
- black tempera paint with a drop of liquid soap (to make it stick)

Motivation:

To communicate thoughts and feelings about the music you hear, using language and a variety of art forms and media

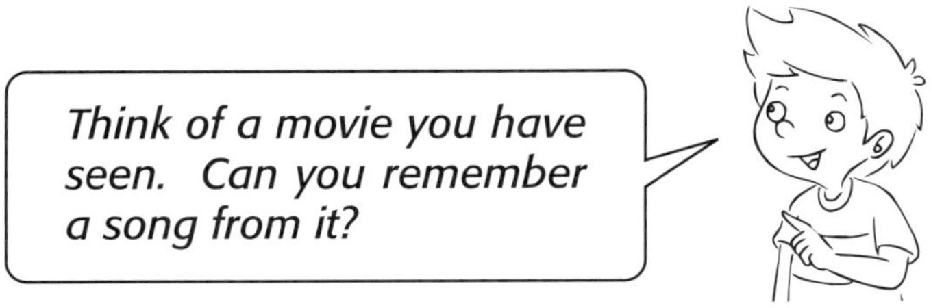

The music of a movie can make it a hit or a failure. The main theme songs from the movies *Chinatown*, *The Godfather*, and *2001: A Space Odyssey* all set a mood. While listening to one of these songs, make a landscape to reflect how it makes you feel.

What to Do:

1. Listen to the song all the way through to get a feeling for the music.
2. Consider the colours that come to mind.
   - Are they warm or cool, bold or muted?
   - Will the paint be heavy or light?
   - Will colours overlap?
3. Use the brush to wet the page.
4. Play the music again while you paint the background (entire page, lighter colours first) to reflect the music's mood. Experiment with a variety of brushstrokes. Use the rag or sponge dipped in watered-down paint to create different effects.
5. While this is drying, use the pencil to draw detailed images on the Styrofoam tray. These will be printed onto your background. You could draw several connected skyscrapers to create a cityscape silhouette. Then cut around the outline of the image.
6. Paint this with black tempera and quickly press onto the background to reveal a print.

Name: Date:

Instrument Families

Objective: *To recognize and classify various instruments*

Instruments are grouped into families because they are related to one another. They often look alike, are made of the same types of materials, and make a sound in the same way.

A clear, triumphant call on a battlefield is usually connected to a specific brass instrument – the trumpet. Instruments of the **brass family** all have a pipe-like centre that widens at the end, like a bell. By buzzing into the special mouthpiece and mastering the valves on the pipes to change the pitch, jazz and big band players bring these instruments to life.

The **string** family is mostly made of wood. Instruments in this family are mostly hollow, allowing sound to vibrate. Musicians move a bow, made with real horse tail hair, across the strings. They may also use their fingers to pluck or hit the strings to create sound.

There is also a family of instruments that you can hit, scrape, or shake! It is called the **percussion** family. Some of these instruments can play a change in pitch and others play the rhythm. A rock band might be lost without its drummer keeping the beat!

Instruments in the **woodwind** family can be made of wood or other materials, like metal. Musicians blow in through the mouthpiece of these narrow pipes and use their fingers to cover the holes to change the pitch.

Making an instrument is an art form and it can take at least 80 hours and 150 parts to make a good one!

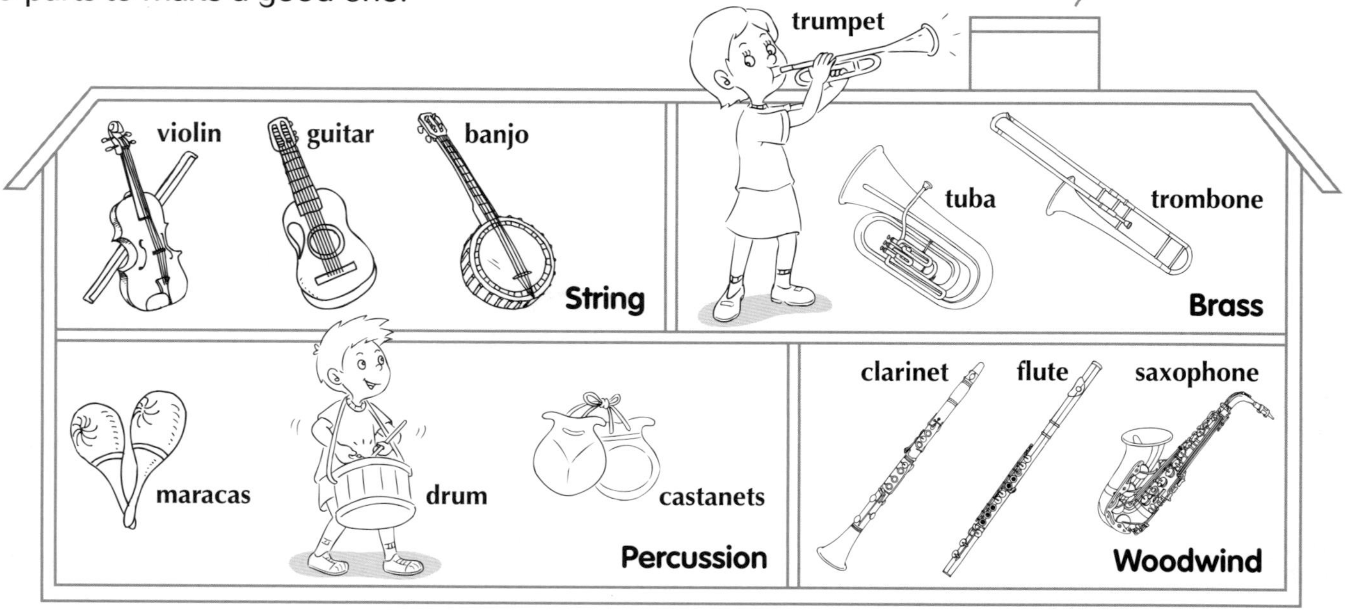

Name: Date:

Instrument Families

Find a picture of a musical instrument from each instrument family in a magazine or newspaper. Then write how the instrument makes music.

1. **Woodwind Instrument** 

____

____

____

2. **Percussion Instrument** 

____

____

____

3. **Stringed Instrument** 

____

____

____

4. **Brass Instrument** 

____

____

____

Name: Date:

Instrument Families

Check the correct answer to see how much you know about each instrument.

1. The harder you hit a drum,

   (A) the louder the sound.

   (B) the higher the pitch of the sound.

   (C) the lower the pitch of the sound.

2. After the drum skin is tightened, the sound the drum makes when struck

   (A) gets lower in pitch.

   (B) gets higher in pitch.

   (C) stays the same.

3. The longer the strings of a stringed instrument,

   (A) the louder the sound.

   (B) the higher the pitch of the sound.

   (C) the lower the pitch of the sound.

4. After the strings are tightened, the sound a stringed instrument makes when plucked

   (A) gets lower in pitch.

   (B) gets higher in pitch.

   (C) stays the same.

Answers: A, B, C, B

Name: Date:

Instrument Families

Making Instruments

Motivation:

To construct and make use of an instrument

Materials:

- paintbrush
- xacto knife
- masking tape
- aluminum foil
- craft paint
- dried beans
- craft spray (sealant)
- 2 oblong-shaped gourds

What to Do:

1. Cut a hole in "bulb" part of gourd. Save the cut-out piece.
2. Scoop out pulp. Let dry overnight.
3. Fill the gourd with 3 tablespoons of dried b
4. Cover the hole with aluminum foil.
5. Cover the aluminum foil with the cut-ou and seal it with masking tape.
6. Paint gourd. Let dry.
7. Spray gourd with craft spray.

Discussion:

- What family does the instrument you have made belong to?
- How do you make sounds with this instrument?

Name: Date:

Making Music

Objective: *To create musical compositions that show appropriate use of some of the elements of music*

Have you ever wondered what it would be like to make your own music?

Have you ever dreamed of having your own band?

Now that you have your own instrument, you can use it to bring words to life...but first let's review the elements of music.

Think of the clear, even beats of your heart. In music, this steady pulse is like the **beat** of the song. If you can clap your hands along to the music, then you are probably clapping to the beat.

Some beats can be longer or shorter than others, making a **rhythm**. Rhythm is the pattern of long and short sounds that is repeated to drive the music forward. *A rum, pitter patter pang, a rum pitter patter pang* is a rhythm.

If you run up a hill, your heart beats faster. In music, this would be like a change in **tempo**. It is the speed of a piece.

When you are frightened, your heart seems to beat loudly. The **dynamics** are the different degrees of volume of a piece.

In music, the sound of a note is called its **pitch**. Groups of notes played one after another are called the **melody** or tune. Think of *Happy Birthday*, hum along, and you've got the melody!

These are the basics that help us create music. An instrument might plunk, honk, clang, or toot. It might be able to create a melody. Perhaps it can play the rhythm or carry the beat. Whatever the sound of an instrument, put your heart into using it, and you'll make music!

Name: Date:

Making Music

A. Write the definition of each term.

1. Melody

____

2. Pitch

____

3. Tempo

____

4. Dynamics

____

5. Tone Colour

____

6. Rhythm

____

B. What kind of music expresses these feelings best?

1. excited and happy

Dynamics: _______________

Tempo: _______________

Tone Colour: _______________

2. sad and blue

Dynamics: _______________

Tempo: _______________

Tone Colour: _______________

Name: Date:

Making Music

Read the pitch of the instruments in each family. Check the appropriate tone colour and instruments that would be a suitable accompaniment for each song. Then write another suitable instrument.

The human voice is also an instrument. It is mostly used to impart text.

Brass Family

- trumpet – high
- trombone – medium
- tuba – low

String Family

- violin – high
- viola – medium
- cello – low

Percussion Family

- triangle – high
- tambourine – medium
- drum – low

Woodwind Family

- flute – high
- oboe – medium
- basson – low

1. **Twinkle Twinkle Little Star**

Tone Colour

- ○ raspy
- ○ brittle
- ○ metallic
- ○ heavy

Instrument

- ○ drum
- ○ violin
- ○ cello
- ○ flute
- ○ tuba
- ○ ________________

2. **O Canada**

Tone Colour

- ○ muted
- ○ bright
- ○ dark
- ○ piercing

Instrument

- ○ trombone
- ○ flute
- ○ triangle
- ○ oboe
- ○ viola
- ○ ________________

Name: Date:

Making Music

Our Own Blues

Materials:

- instruments

Motivation:

To create an accompaniment for a story, poem, or drama presentation

The "Blues" is a type of music created by enslaved Africans who lived in the southern U.S. They worked very hard and expressed the terrible troubles they experienced through the lyrics and rhythm of their songs.

What to Do:

1 Read this together with expression, noticing the rhythm.

Down, down baby, down by the roller coaster.
Sweet, sweet baby, I'll never let you go.
Shimmy, shimmy cocoa puff,
Shimmy shimmy pow!
Shimmy, Shimmy cocoa puff,
Shimmy shimmy pow...

2 This time, use your instrument to create an accompaniment.

- Will your instrument carry the rhythm or the beat?
- Can you play a melody?
- Which parts will be faster or louder?

3 Do it again, adjusting the tempo and dynamics. What tone colour will this song have?

4 The twelve-bar blues is just twelve measures of four beats each. This is 48 claps. Use different instruments to create a 48 beat, twelve-bar blues. Try finding some instruments to make these sounds.

Twang : 8 beats
Blow : 8 beats
Shake : 8 beats
Snap : 8 beats
Tap : 4 beats
Shake : 8 beats
Clap : 4 beats

5 Get into groups of four or five students. Decide who will be the singer(s) while you all play along with your instruments. How will the melody and rhythm go?

Art Lessons
Grades **5-6**

Visual Arts

Name: Date:

Colour Relationship – a Basic Colour Wheel

Objective: *To identify and name the primary and secondary colours and recognize some tints and shades of colours*

All the colours in the world come from just three **primary** colours: red, yellow, and blue. These colours are primary because they are not produced by mixing other colours together. Interestingly, the human eye has these three colour receptors in the retina – the light sensitive surface of your eyes.

You would be surprised to find that virtually all the colours we see are based on these three primary colours. When any of these primary colours are mixed at a time, **secondary** colours – orange (red + yellow), green (blue + yellow), and purple (red + blue), are created.

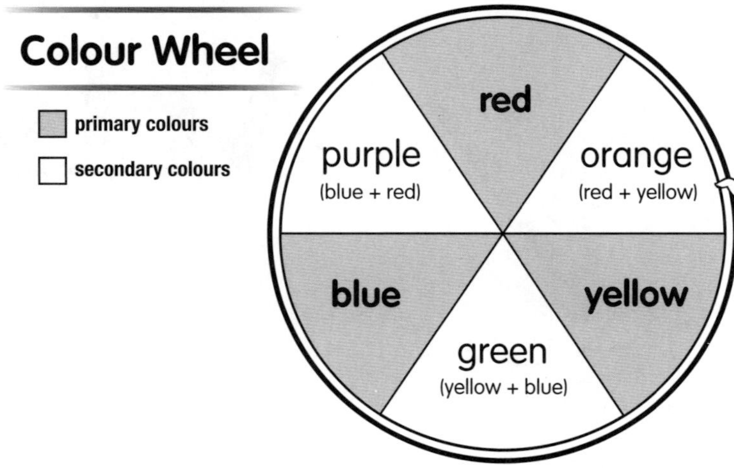

Also, any colour mixed with one of the 2 **neutrals** – white or black – results in a **tint** (any colour + white) or a **shade** (any colour + black).

Tint Colours: any colour + white

e.g. red + white = pink
blue + white = baby blue

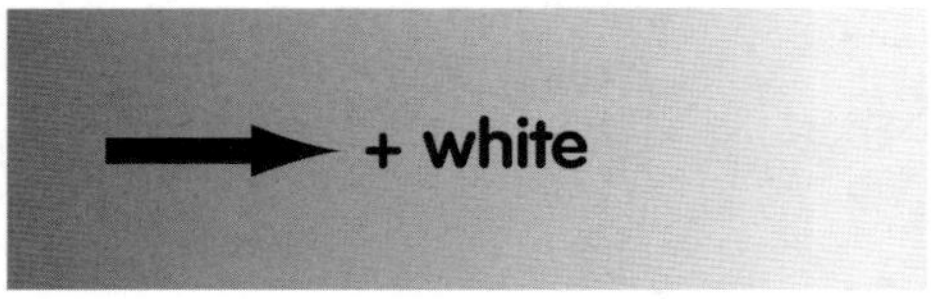

Shade Colours: any colour + black

e.g. blue + black = navy blue
orange + black = dark orange

Name: Date:

Colour Relationship – a Basic Colour Wheel

Answer the questions.

1. What are the primary colours?

____

2. What are the secondary colours? How can they be made?

____

____

3. What are the two neutrals?

____

____

4. What are tints?

____

____

5. What are shades?

____

____

6. Colour the boxes to show a tint and a shade of red.

Tint of Red

Shade of Red

Name: Date:

Colour Relationship – a Basic Colour Wheel

Make a colour wheel to show the primary colours, secondary colours, and shades of those colours.

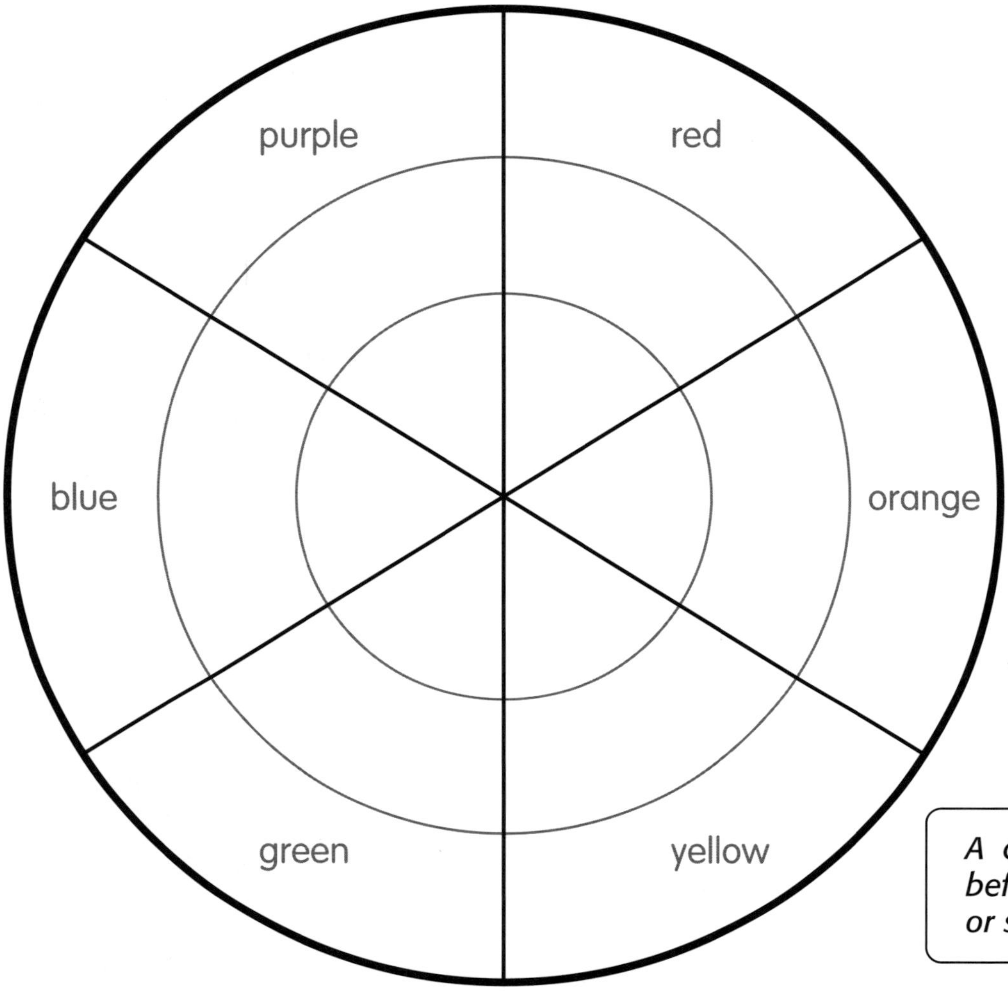

Steps:

1. Start with red, yellow, and blue paints – the primary colours – to colour the outermost sections.
2. Add a bit of black to each primary colour and colour each middle section with that shade. Then add a bit of black again to colour the innermost sections. This will show shades of the primary colours.
3. Mix two primary colours to make a secondary colour.
4. Add a bit of black to each secondary colour to make shades as in step 2 to finish your beautiful colour wheel.

Name: Date:

Colour Relationship – a Basic Colour Wheel

Materials:

- 8.5 x 11″ white paper or Bristol board
- scissors
- glue stick
- variety of materials (three primary colours plus black and white)
  - ☐ coloured pencils
  - ☐ poster paints
  - ☐ paint colour chips
  - ☐ pastels/crayons
  - ☐ magazine photos
  - ☐ coloured construction paper

Motivation:

To design your own basic colour wheel using different materials

What to Do:

1. Choose your materials (a combination of different materials could produce more interesting results).

2. Draw the basic framework for your chart on the Bristol board. Below are some examples of interesting charts.

e.g. 1

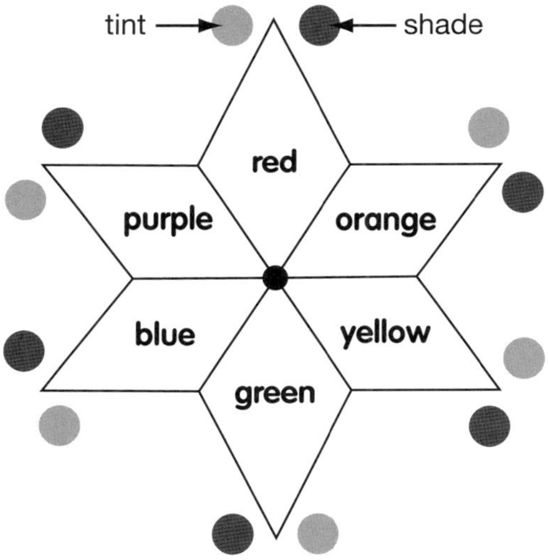

* Tint on the left and shade on the right

e.g. 2

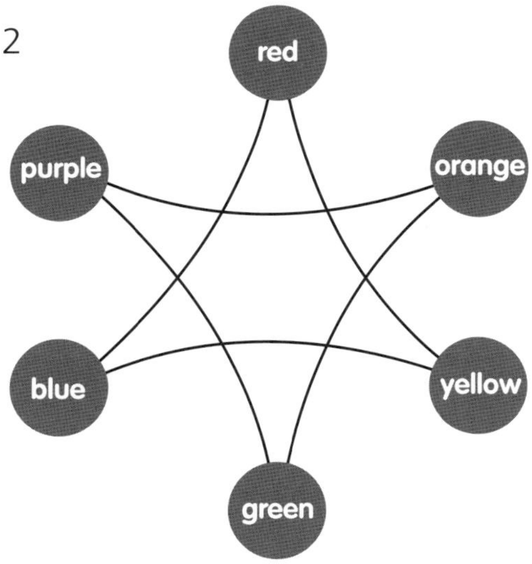

3. Complete the colour wheel using your choice of materials.

4. Display your results.

Name: Date:

Complementary Colours

Objective: *To identify and name the complementary colours*

Do you think you would be comfortably resting in a bedroom that was painted yellow and purple?

Do you think you would prefer a bedroom that was painted light blue or pink?

Designing art work and rooms with colour has taken place worldwide for centuries. One type of colour combination often used is called **low contrast** (*very little difference*) or **monochromatic**. A typical example of **monochrome** (*mono* = one, *chrome* = colour) would be a design, work of art, or interior coloured completely blue with different tints (white plus a small amount of blue) or shades (blue plus a small amount of black).

Complementary colours are the direct opposites of monochromatic colours. Complementary colours are in **high contrast** (great difference) and are opposite on the colour wheel, like yellow and purple. There are three pairs of complementary colours on a basic colour wheel – red and green, yellow and purple, and blue and orange.

Colour Wheel

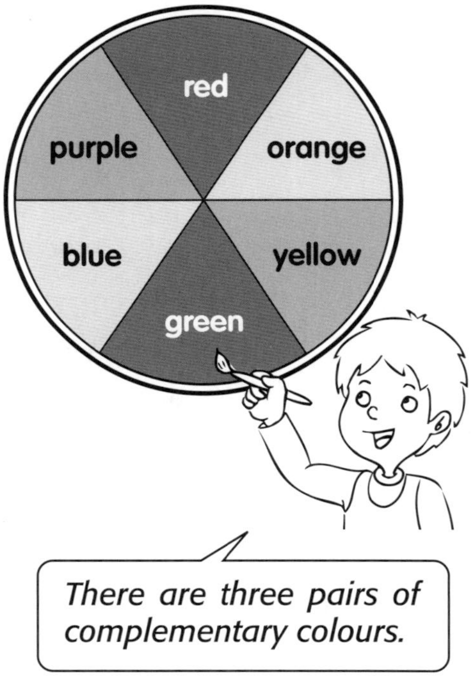

Throughout history, complementary colours have been used for seasons and cultural celebrations. A typical example of this would be red (*a primary*) and green (*a secondary*). We see lots of red and green during Christmas celebrations, and at Easter, purple and yellow are often used.

These high contrast colours (opposites) are exciting, full of action, and attract attention. The complementary combinations are in such great contrast that our eyes are not able to deal with the "vibrating" edges between them. Examples of this are circus objects like the seats on a Ferris wheel or the animals on a carousel. This is why you probably would not want a restful place, like your bedroom, to be painted yellow and purple.

Name: Date:

Complementary Colours

Colour the rings and the circles with the specified colours. Then fill in the blanks. Notice how some combinations have more contrast, making them stand out.

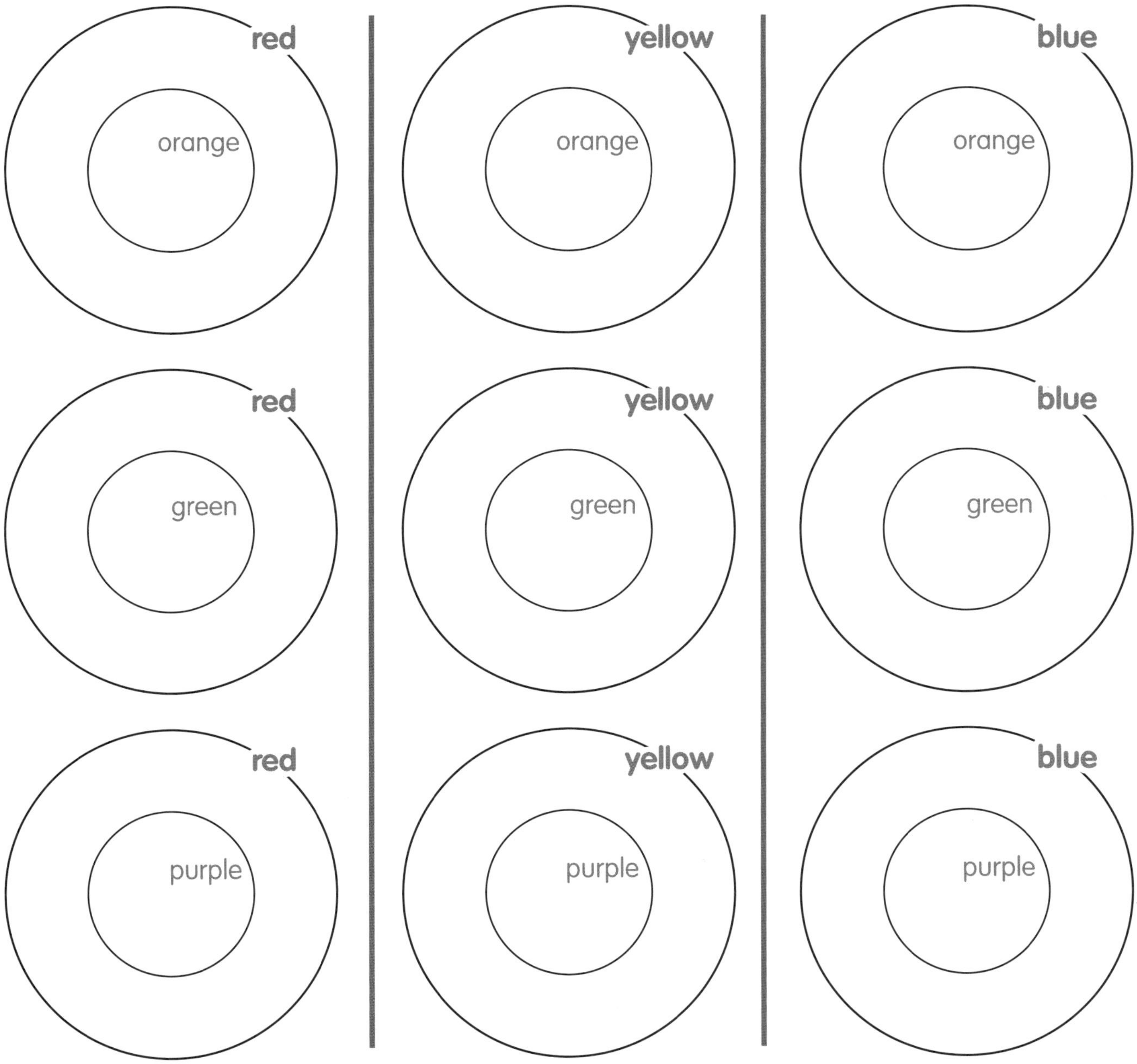

Complementary Colours

- red and ____________________
- yellow and ____________________
- blue and ____________________

Name: Date:

Complementary Colours

Use the complementary colours associated with Christmas and Easter to colour the pictures.

Name: Date:

Complementary Colours

Materials:

- 8.5 x 11″ paper
- string
- sticks or dowels
- scissors
- hole punch
- coloured pencils or paints

Motivation:

Make a mobile with any shapes, using only two complementary colours that show excitement and movement

What to Do:

1. Trace nine identical shapes (squares, circles, or stars) on the white paper.
2. Draw some patterns on both sides of the shapes and colour the sections with two complementary colours.

e.g.

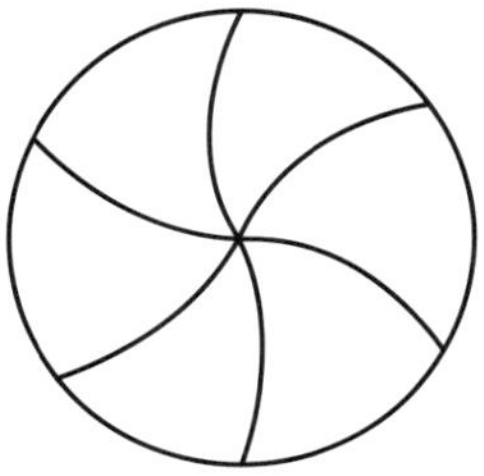

Shape: circle

Pattern: spiral

Colour: yellow and purple

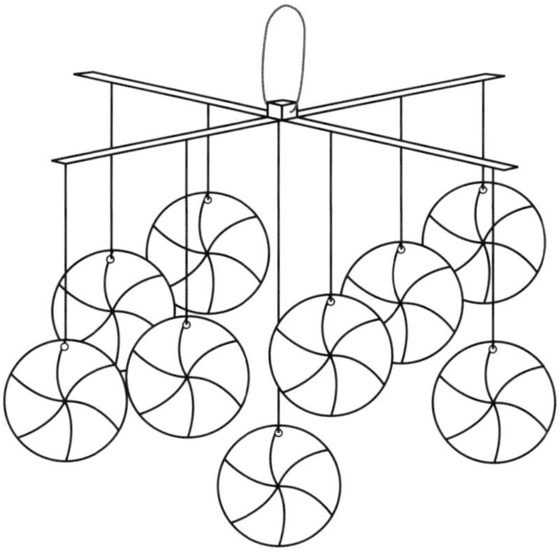

3. Cut out the shapes.
4. Punch a hole in the shape and thread the string through the hole.
5. Tie the other end of the string to the stick.
6. Attach the other shapes in the same way.
7. Balance the shapes to make a mobile.

Tip:

Students might write a paragraph explaining why using only complementary colours works well to attract attention to their design or graphic work.

Name: Date:

Art and Its Surroundings

Objective: *To recognize and describe the relationship between a work of art and its surroundings*

Can you imagine what your classroom would look like if no one cared where anything was?

What if all the desks were pushed into a corner, the teacher's desk was piled on top, and all the books and classroom materials were dumped onto the pile of furniture?

An object's surroundings are very important. Even creatures of the animal kingdom are concerned about where they put things. Spiders, beavers, and eagles all have certain places for their valued objects. Like animals, people also have specific places for things. We are mindful of where we put furniture and pictures in each of the rooms in our house. Things are not shoved into a room and just left there; they are arranged in ways that seem to look best.

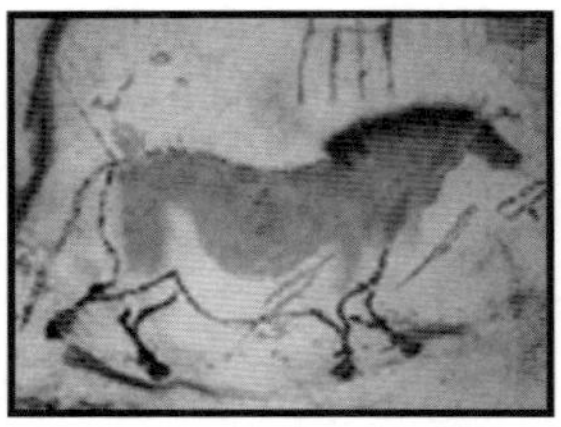
Cave Paintings of Lascaux

Some mistakes in placing art would be: hanging pictures up-side-down, hanging pictures over windows, or gluing pictures up on the ceiling. We do not do any of these things because doing so would take away from one's experience with the piece of art. Creating a disconnection between a piece of art and its surroundings usually works against the message the artist is trying to convey through his or her art.

The Academy of Athens

St. Peter's Square, Vatican City

Throughout history, artists and architects (people who design buildings) have used great care and concern in arranging their works. The idea of creating harmony between a piece of art and its surroundings is not new; the ancient Greeks and Romans took great care in arranging their works of art indoors as well as outdoors. Next time you take a trip to any large city, observe how artists and planners have made things look their best by considering the relationship between a work of art and its surroundings.

Royal Ontario Museum

Name: Date:

Art and Its Surroundings

Circle the answer that would be the best surrounding for each type of art.

1. **A Landscape Painting**

   A. hung on the wall next to other paintings with the same theme

   B. put on the floor next to a chair

   C. hung on the wall in a dark room

2. **A Large Abstract Sculpture**

   A. in a small room

   B. in a large room on its own

   C. in a large room filled with landscape paintings

3. **A Small Figurine**

   A. in a large room with giant sculptures

   B. in a glass case with similar figurines

   C. in a glass case with live animals

4. **Print Art**

   A. hidden away in a filing cabinet

   B. displayed in a frame, on the wall in a room with soft lighting

   C. taped to the front of a bathroom door

Name: Date:

Art and Its Surroundings

Which piece of art would be best appropriate for the following institutions or places? Write your answer and explain your choice on the lines.

1. **A City Park**

Different Kinds of Art

- monument
- student-made mural
- sculpture of a holy figure
- statues of ancient people

2. **A School Foyer**

3. **A Classic Museum**

4. **A Church**

Name: Date:

Art and Its Surroundings

Materials:

- decorative paper or wallpaper samples
- shoeboxes, tissue boxes, or milk cartons
- scissors
- glue stick
- coloured construction paper
- plasticine
- magazines
- Bristol board

Motivation:

To make a diorama of an art gallery room using pictures, murals, and sculptures

What to Do:

1. Put the shoebox or tissue box on the table with the top side open.
2. Make two doors and one window.
3. Line the inside walls of your gallery room with the best colour for your display. (Remember to choose colours that go well with the objects in your gallery.)
4. Pick at least five pictures from magazines and cut them out.
5. Make a frame for each picture you have cut out.
6. Make at least three stands and sculptures for your display.
7. If you have time, make another version, with similar objects and a different arrangement in a similar gallery room.

* Remember to consider carefully the relationships between the objects, their colours, sizes, frames, and where they are placed in your gallery room.

Name: Date:

Installing Sculptures

Objective: *To identify the things to be considered when placing a sculpture*

Why do you put things where you do?

Do you ever put something somewhere because you think it looks good there?

What are some of the reasons for the choices you make when placing a favoured object somewhere?

There are many things to be considered before installing a sculpture. Before taking action, you have to make decisions about the action you will perform. When installing a work of art, several choices need to be considered. Installing a sculpture is very much like deciding where to put something like a lamp or a dresser in your bedroom.

Things you need to take into consideration include: where it would look best, where it would be viewed best, and what the best lighting would be. Can you see how these questions are closely related to the kinds of decisions you would make when placing objects in your own home?

Some decisions would probably not be made because they are silly, impractical, and do not compliment the objects you are installing. For instance, setting a sculpture directly on the floor would not be a good idea if it is the size of a milk carton. Likewise, a large sculpture would probably not be well displayed in a small room or on a compact shelf.

Size, direction, colour, lighting, and height are all things to be considered when installing a sculpture.

Name: Date:

Installing Sculptures

A. Check the things to be considered when placing a sculpture.

- (A) size
- (B) direction
- (C) gender
- (D) texture
- (E) lighting
- (F) flexibility
- (G) how high it should be placed
- (H) if the object is liked or not

B. Decide which things are out of place in the picture. Colour the out-of-place items red. Then discuss with your classmates why you have picked those items.

Name: Date:

Installing Sculptures

Find pictures of the following types of sculptures from magazines, newspapers, or the Internet. Cut them out and glue them in the appropriate spaces. Then write where you would install these pieces and why.

A Plant Sculpture	**A Relief Sculpture**
A Monument	**A Bust – sculpture of a head**

A Plant Sculpture: ____________________

____

A Relief Sculpture: ____________________

____

A Monument: ____________________

____

A Bust – sculpture of a head: ____________________

____

Name: Date:

Installing Sculptures

Materials:

- a shoebox, tissue box, or small cardboard box
- paper and pencils
- plasticine in different colours
- Bristol board
- Scotch tape and masking tape
- scissors

Motivation:

To consider and design a model of a room interior with special concern for where the objects are placed and where they would look best

What to Do:

1 Draw a line around the box you plan to use for your diorama on a sheet of paper.

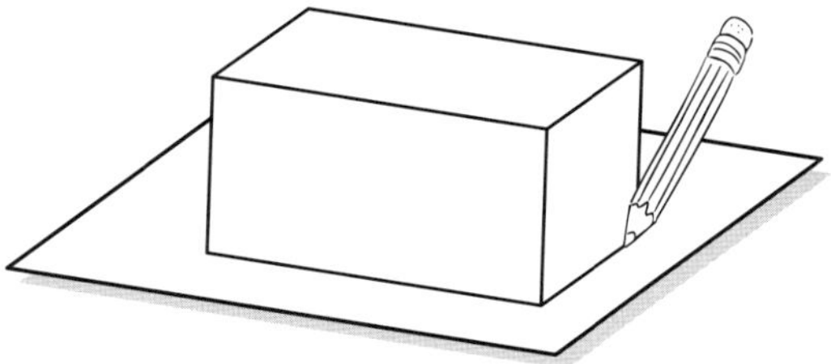

2 Draw a floor plan of where you want to place your doors, windows, stands, sculptures, and light fixtures. Your room should have two doors, two windows, and at least five light fixtures.

e.g.

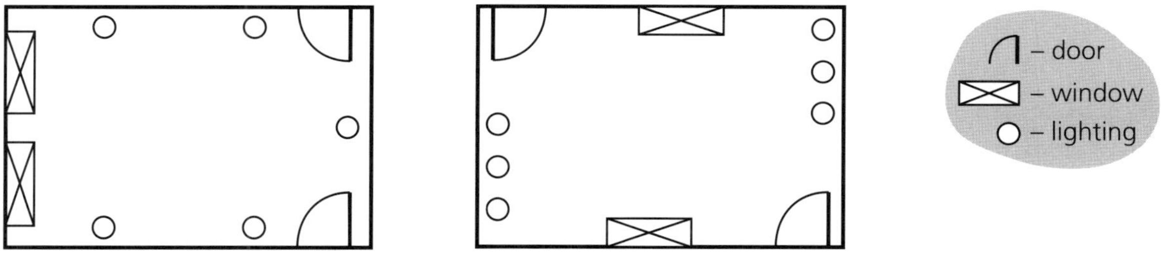

3 Consider a theme for your display, for instance, animals, people, insects, or plants. Make little plasticine model sculptures of your choice.

4 Make little stands for sculptures where needed by taping Bristol board into cylinders or rectangles.

5 Begin with the open box to place the stands and sculptures in the positions you have decided on your floor plan.

6 Make little model spotlights or light fixtures and tape them to the gallery walls in the positions you chose on your floor plan.

7 Put your sculptures in place, on the stands positioned according to your floor plan design.

Name: Date:

Creating Texture

Objective: *To identify tools and techniques used by artists to create texture*

Can you name an art tool and what it is used for?

Can you name a texture and tell how it is made?

Do you think a person who is visually impaired would be able to identify texture?

If so, how?

Textures have been used by painters and sculptors diversely throughout history. Both visual and physical textures are used by artists in different ways to express emotion or to convey a message. Physical textures can be rough or smooth, while visual textures can only appear rough or smooth.

There are many ways of creating texture; mostly, tools are used to produce the effect. Tools are used by artists to create illusory texture as well as physical texture. For every different material, whether paint on canvas, wood, or stone, a special tool is used on or with it to create various kinds of textures. Similarly, every kind of texture is created by means of a special technique that is applied with this specific kind of tool.

Each of these paints is able to create a different kind of texture.

Oil Paint – This is a slow-drying paint that is said to have a translucent texture similar to that of human skin.

Watercolour Paint – This paint is used in combination with a solvent and can create an airy, lucid texture.

Gouache – This is a heavy, opaque paint that has great reflective qualities and can be used to represent shiny textures.

Acrylic Paint – This fast-drying paint has a glossy finish and can be used to create smooth textures.

Name: Date:

Creating Texture

A. **Name three objects that have the following textures. Write them on the lines.**

rough	smooth	furry	prickly

B. **For each indicated texture, think of an object with that texture and draw it in the box. Then use different tools and colours to make its texture appear realistic.**

rough

smooth

furry

prickly

Name: Date:

Creating Texture

Glue a different textured material in each box. Recreate the materials you have chosen by drawing them in the "My Artwork" space. Then write which tools or techniques you used to recreate the texture of these materials.

My Artwork

Tools / Techniques Used:

My Artwork

Tools / Techniques Used:

Name: Date:

Creating Texture

Materials:

- a magazine picture of a work of art (a painting, drawing, print, or sculpture)
- pamphlets from art museums
- advertisements for local gallery
- calendars (with art themed pictures)

Motivation:

To write a short paper expressing your ideas about art tools and the illusion of texture

What to Do:

1. Look carefully at the pictures you chose from those your teacher has provided for you. Choose one to use for your project.

2. Stop and look quietly at your picture, at its details, colours, highlights, shades, and shadows. Pay special attention to the areas of your picture that have or demonstrate texture.

3. Remember that texture has a particular surface, and notice whether things are smooth or rough, choppy or bumpy.

4. Start writing your paper; don't forget to identify the work of art you have chosen. Include the name of the work, the name of the artist, and the date it was made. You can add its location or the art gallery it is in as well.

5. Give a brief description of what the picture is of, for example, horses in a field near a barn. Then comment on what the condition seems to be, whether it is nice weather or if it is stormy. Finally, identify the areas of the picture where textures have been used.

horses in a field near a barn on a sunny day

Name: Date:

The Textures of Emotion

Objective: *To describe how artists use texture to represent or evoke an emotional response*

Have you ever laughed or cried at a movie?

Have you ever become happy, sad, or angry because of a painting you saw?

Artists throughout the ages have been able to include feeling in their art work by means of texture. They have used many materials, techniques, colours, textures, shapes, and forms to stir up a viewer's emotions.

Art can demonstrate a variety of moods and feelings. For example, some art works are made with very bright colours to emphasize joyfulness; others are black, white, and darkly lit to emphasize feelings of melancholy and sadness.

Here are some of the ways artists manipulate the effects of texture to represent emotions:

By Changing Colours:

- bright colours and tints for cheerfulness
- dark colours and shades for gloom

By Using Lines:

thin, delicate lines for light and airiness

dark and thick lines for sadness or gloom

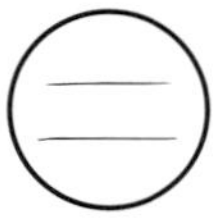

horizontal lines for peace and calm

diagonal lines for excitement and movement

curved and wiggly lines for suspense and fear

Name: Date:

The Textures of Emotion

Answer each of the following questions by checking the correct letter. Then create an illustration of the answer in the space provided.

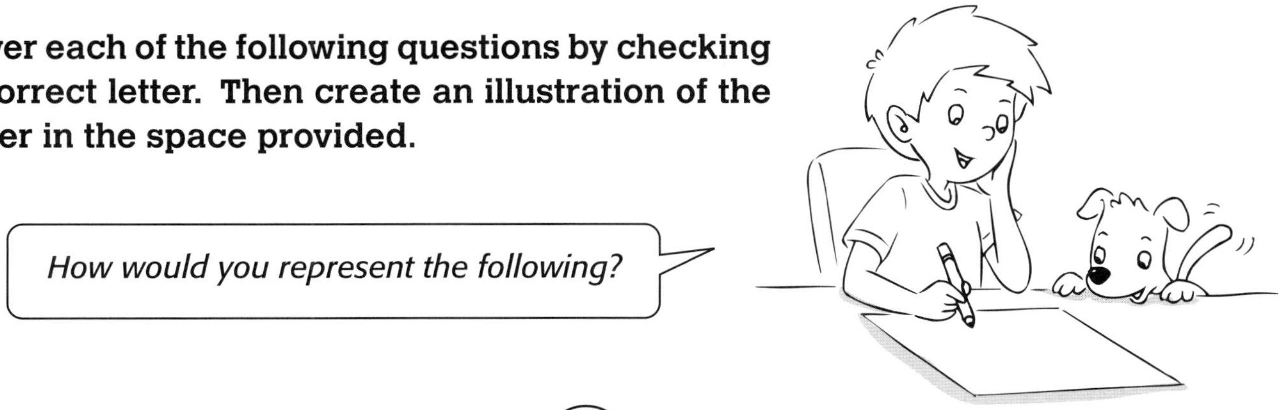

1. **Fright / Suspense**
   - A straight lines
   - B wiggly lines
   - C broken lines

2. **Sadness**
   - A bright colours
   - B dark, thick lines
   - C diagonal lines

3. **Tranquility**
   - A light, horizontal lines
   - B dark colours
   - C heavy, continuous lines

4. **Excitement**
   - A thin, delicate lines
   - B shades
   - C diagonal lines

Name: Date:

The Textures of Emotion

Colour the pictures using the colours indicated. Use light, straight, wiggly, thick, delicate, or other lines to add effects while colouring. Then give three emotions describing the mood created by each colour scheme.

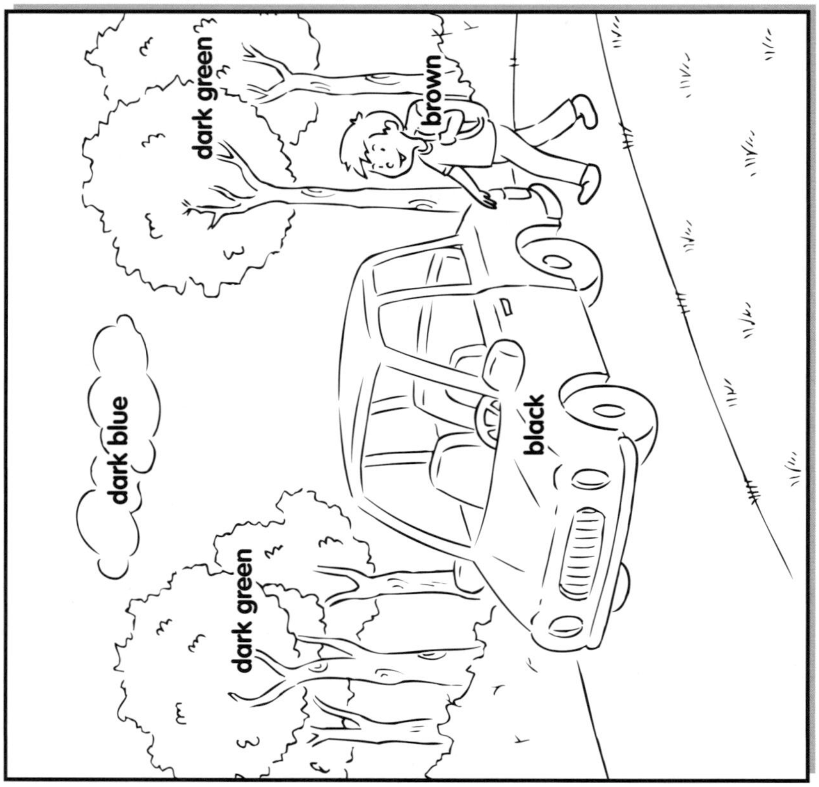

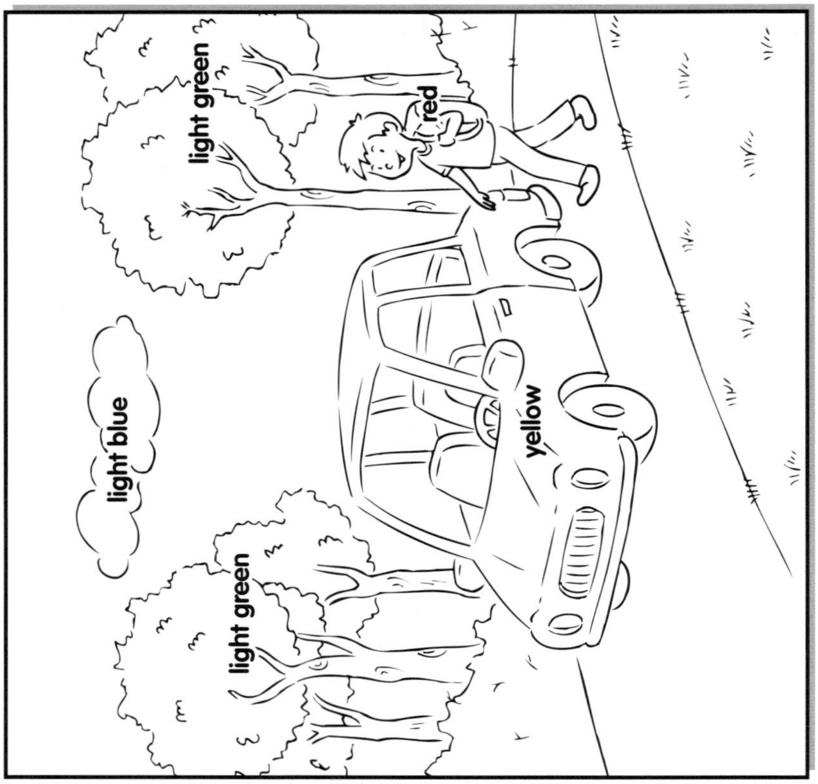

Name: Date:

The Textures of Emotion

Materials:

- 11 x 17″ Bristol board
- poster paints and brushes
- coloured pencils, pastels, and crayons
- ruler
- found materials

Motivation:

To use a specific subject and technique to evoke an emotion

a) Choose a subject for your picture, for example, the circus, a car race, or a flower show. Choose a mood to go with this subject, for example, a happy circus, a fast moving car race, or a delicate flower show. Use a specific technique to express the mood you have chosen. For example, use thin lines for the delicate flower show.

b) Make the same themed picture again, only this time change the mood. For example, change the flower show from delicate to bold using bright colours to represent cheer and diagonal lines to show action.

What to Do:

1. Choose a theme for your picture, for example, the circus.
2. Draw the basic outline of your idea on the Bristol board in light pencil.
3. Choose a mood to portray in your picture, for example, happiness.
4. Choose a technique to illustrate this feeling.
5. Use the materials you think will work best to show the emotions you want to portray.
6. Complete one picture and if you have more time, do the same picture and subject with a different mood.

A Circus

- balloon – felt
- clown – construction paper
- cloud – cotton
- kids – colourful pictures from magazines
- strings – yarn
- tent – cloth

Name: Date:

The Strengths and Limitations in Making Art

Objective: *To describe the strengths and limitations of various art tools, materials, and techniques*

What is the best tool you could use to drive a nail into a block of wood?

What is better for painting the walls of your room, a 1" brush or a 12" paint roller?

Do you think the best way to paint a car is with a brush, roller, or spray gun?

When making decisions about the best material, tool, or technique to use for a job, you need to consider its *strengths* (the positive things) and *limitations* (the negative things).

Some materials are more difficult and complicated to work with than others. For example, working with various types of stone requires hard and sharp steel chisels, files, and rasps; this can be seen as a limitation. The hard and durable composition of stone – a strength, requires tools that are very different from those needed to create works made out of copper. Copper is much softer than stone and can be formed into shapes that do not break off easily. Once you break a piece of stone, it cannot be repaired, whereas if you break a piece of copper, it can be welded back together.

Tools used to create "flat" art also have strengths and limitations. Covering a large canvas with paint using a tiny paintbrush intended for small details would be very tiring and time consuming. Moreover, trying to capture the intricate details of a landscape would be nearly impossible if you used a large, flat brush intended for spreading paint. In this unit, you will learn about the strengths and limitations of a variety of tools, materials, and techniques by using those tools to perform identical tasks. You will make a list of each tool's strengths and limitations, demonstrating that not all tools perform the same way.

Name: Date:

The Strengths and Limitations in Making Art

Circle either "strength" or "limitation" for each of the following art tools. Explain your choice.

1. 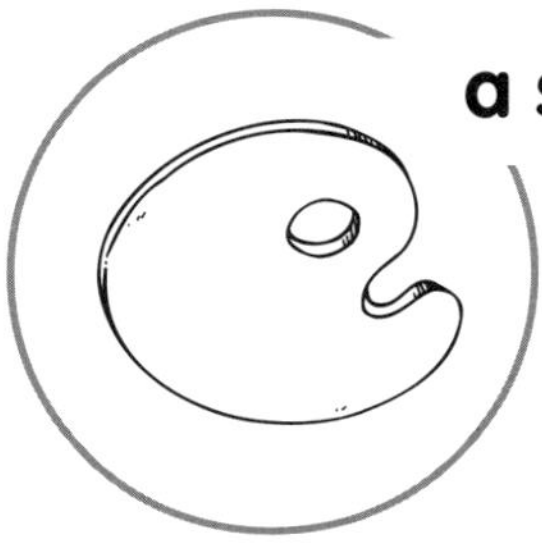

a small palette – strength / limitation

____

____

2. 

black and white film – strength / limitation

____

____

3. 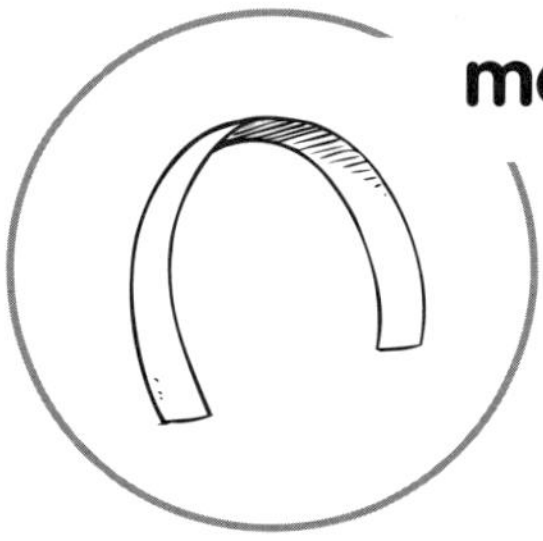

metal that bends easily – strength / limitation

____

____

4. 

a sharp and sturdy carving knife – strength / limitation

____

____

5. 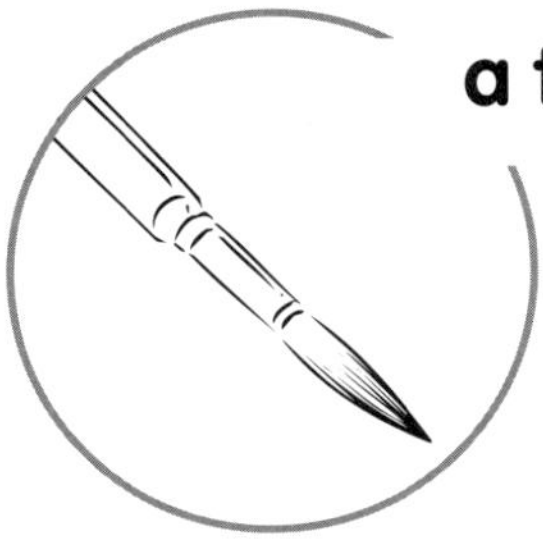

a thin paintbrush – strength / limitation

____

____

Name: Date:

The Strengths and Limitations in Making Art

Colour the common tools used for creating the following works of art.

1. A large, free-standing sculpture made of marble

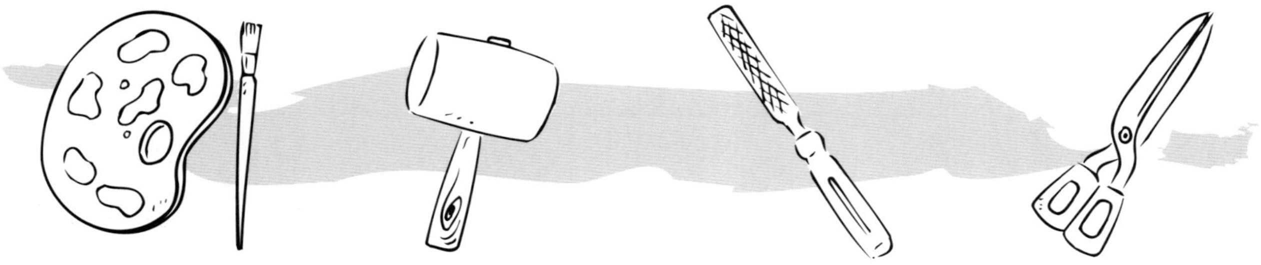

2. A collage made of magazine clippings

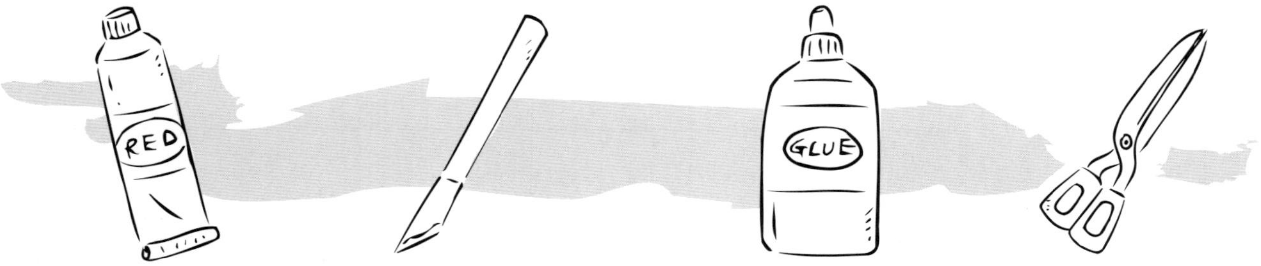

3. An oil painting

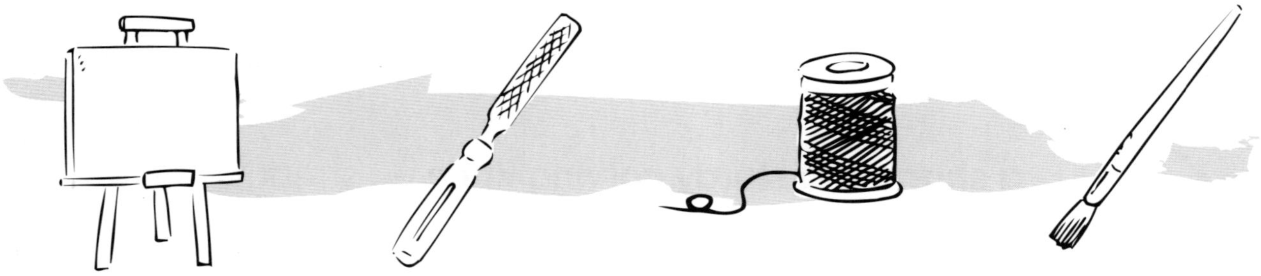

4. A cave painting

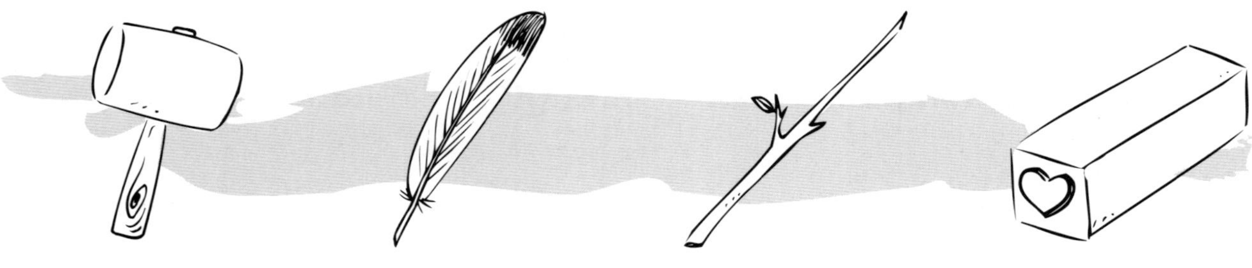

Name: Date:

The Strengths and Limitations in Making Art

Materials:

- different coloured tempera paints
- 3 different tools to apply paint:
  - sponges
  - small paintbrushes
  - fan brush
- 3 pieces of paper with the same image on them (tree, bear, person, etc.)

Motivation:

To learn the strengths and limitations of art tools by using different tools to perform the same task

What to Do:

1. Distribute one of each kind of painting tool per child.
2. Set up the paint, painting tools, and paper with the image on it.
3. Apply the paint to the image without surpassing the lines. Use a different painting tool for each image.
4. When all three images have been painted, write about the strengths and limitations of each tool. Describe how easy or difficult it was to use the sponge to make details or to use the small brush to cover a large area. Describe the techniques you used, and which worked best with what tool.

e.g.

Name: Date:

Tools, Materials, and Techniques

Objective: *To be able to select the most appropriate tools, materials, and techniques for a particular purpose and use them correctly*

Did you know that one of the most famous artists of all time, Leonardo da Vinci, made serious mistakes in choosing the materials and techniques to make one of his most well-known paintings?

Some have said that the creation of Leonardo da Vinci's *Last Supper* (1498), a very large mural in Milan, Italy, was not very well thought through. Instead of creating a traditional fresco (a painting on wet plaster on a wall), the artist invented a new paint that was mixed with wax to craft his images. The result was a mess. The paint would not dry properly, and it began to melt off the wall when he attempted to dry it with fires lit in front of the painting.

Making good choices about the materials and tools used to create a work has always been a very important part of producing art. Any new or different ideas require experimentation before they can be identified as having more strengths than limitations.

Jackson Pollock's painting technique was not only unique, but also innovative, as not many had used pouring and dripping as a method of applying paint to a canvas before. His technique wasn't the only thing that was unconventional; the materials he used for his "drip" paintings were as well! Pollock is said to have used household paint instead of artists' paint to create some of his works.

Today, there are as many ways of creating art as there are types (genres) of art. There are so many that the question, "How is this art?" often arises. Although there are no set rules on how to manipulate materials, tools, and techniques to create art, their application is often most successful when following the suggested, traditional methods of use.

But who is to say that with a little experimentation, a new, better way of using a certain tool, material, or technique won't be discovered? Who knows, some day one of you might be the one to discover it!

Last Supper
Leonardo da Vinci, 1498

Name: Date:

Tools, Materials, and Techniques

Check the tools you think would work best to create each piece of art. Then give reasons for your choice.

1. **Painting a Mural**

(A) toothbrush

(B) hairbrush

(C) paintbrush

Reason: ____________________

____

____

2. **Wood Working**

(A) cheese knife

(B) carving knife

(C) sand paper

Reason: ____________________

____

____

3. **Large Marble Sculpture**

(A) chisel

(B) easel

(C) hammer

Reason: ____________________

____

____

Name: Date:

Tools, Materials, and Techniques

Find pictures of the materials below from old magazines or newspapers. Cut them out and glue them in the appropriate spaces. Then, consider the given techniques and write which would be used to manipulate each material.

Technique

moulding blowing paint pouring

cross-stitching carving hammer and point work

Fabric: ________________	Paint: ________________
Stone: ________________	Wood: ________________
Clay: ________________	Glass: ________________

Name: Date:

Tools, Materials, and Techniques

Motivation:

To design a themed image (undersea creatures, planets and stars, plants and flowers, race cars, musical instruments, a sport, etc.) and to make a mosaic on a 8.5 x 11" Bristol board using the appropriate tools, materials, and techniques

Materials:

- pencil, ruler, and compass
- 8.5 x 11" paper, Bristol board, and carbon paper
- white glue and glue stick
- various types of pasta noodles and rice
- various types and colours of peas, beans, and grains
- coloured paper cut into small bits, representing tiles or glass
- pieces of coloured felt, cloth, or other left over materials

What to Do:

1. Students should first discuss with their teacher the theme or subject matter for their mosaic and the best tools, materials, and techniques for their mosaic.

2. Draw a rough draft of the design, correcting your mistakes first. When the image is complete, transfer it to the Bristol board using carbon paper.

3. Apply your chosen materials using the best tools and techniques based on the discussion you had with the teacher.

e.g.

Emperor Justinian
from Mosaic Justinian and his retinue
547 CE by San Vitale, Ravenna

Name: Date:

Effects of Art

Objective: *To identify the most appropriate tools, materials, and techniques for a particular purpose*

Have you noticed that the lighting is often very dark when something mysterious or dangerous is happening in a movie or TV program?

Artists always use unique tools and materials to create pottery, paintings, architecture, or sculptures. Creating art requires that artists make decisions about the message of their work ahead of time – what they are trying to express, and what they want the viewer to realize, understand, or feel about their work. When the planning stage is over, artists choose the appropriate tools and materials they will use to create effects that will convey their intended message.

examples of facial expressions

The effects a work of art can have on its audience could be happy or sad, ordinary or surprising, simple or complicated, or shocking or peaceful. Whatever the effect, a work of art always has an intended message.

A certain opinion, feeling, attitude, or emotion in a work of art can be conveyed by using certain colours or techniques that will make the observer feel a certain way. One example is through the use of facial expressions; whether the subject of a painting is happy, sad, angry, suspicious, or confused has a big effect on the art observer. Each face has a different "look" and emotion that can be read by the observer. What effect do you think a portrait of a sad woman in a dark and vacant house would have on you?

The Child's Bath
Mary Cassatt, 1893

Fur Traders on the Missouri
George Caleb Bingham, 1845

Name: Date:

Effects of Art

First fill in the spaces provided with the indicated colour. Then write how it makes you feel and describe an image that comes to mind when you think of each colour. What effect would these colours have on your mood if you saw them in a painting?

1. **Light Blue**

How I Feel / Things I See:

2. **Yellow**

How I Feel / Things I See:

3. **Red**

How I Feel / Things I See:

4. **Green**

How I Feel / Things I See:

Name: Date:

Effects of Art

Describe the message being conveyed in each of the following illustrations by identifying the mood and the effects used to communicate it.

1.

Mood: sad / happy / angry

Effects: It makes me feel relaxed / furious and unstable / peaceful .

2.

Mood: ____________________

Effects: ____________________

____

____

3.

Mood: ____________________

Effects: ____________________

____

____

Name: Date:

Effects of Art

Motivation:

To make a paper-maché mask that will have a specific effect (certain expression or emotion)

Using a balloon as the basic size and form of a head, I will form a mask with newspaper strips dipped into flour paste with repeated applications.

Materials:

- pencil and paper, ruler and compass to make the preliminary design
- balloons of various sizes to accommodate different sizes and shapes of heads
- Bristol board and toilet paper rolls for parts
- newspaper cut into strips
- basins, flour, and water (made into a sticky paste)
- paints, inks, and brushes to paint the final form
- variety of materials (if the mask will have a mosaic surface)

What to Do:

Day 1

1. Draw the plans for your mask on a piece of paper – include the colours, textures, patterns, and designs to be used.
2. Blow up a balloon.
3. Apply repeated layers of newspaper strips to the balloon. Apply the wadded paper or folded Bristol board to the balloon to make parts, such as the nose and ears.
4. Continue adding paper and glue until the face mask is made in the form that expresses your desired effect.

Day 2

5. After allowing the mask to dry, apply texture, colour, and other materials to create your effect.

Name: Date:

Producing Two-dimensional Works of Art

Objective: *To recognize and produce two-dimensional works of art*

Papyrus Ani Curs hiero
hieroglyphs

What is a dimension and what does the phrase two-dimensional mean?

The two dimensions are height (distance from top to bottom) and width (distance from side to side). Together they are known as shape.

Ijazah Arabic
calligraphy certificate

Artists did not always know about the third dimension. In the centuries before the third dimension was used in art, paintings looked flat and were referred to as design, pattern, and decoration.

At different times and in different cultures, designs in flat, two-dimensional works of art were very common. You might be surprised, but some of the first examples of two-dimensional works of art were actually writing systems. Egyptian hieroglyphics (small pictures of objects placed side by side to represent names, words, and ideas) and traditional Chinese writing were two-dimensional designs used for decoration as well as communication. Even today, these design works are not only informative but also beautiful to look at!

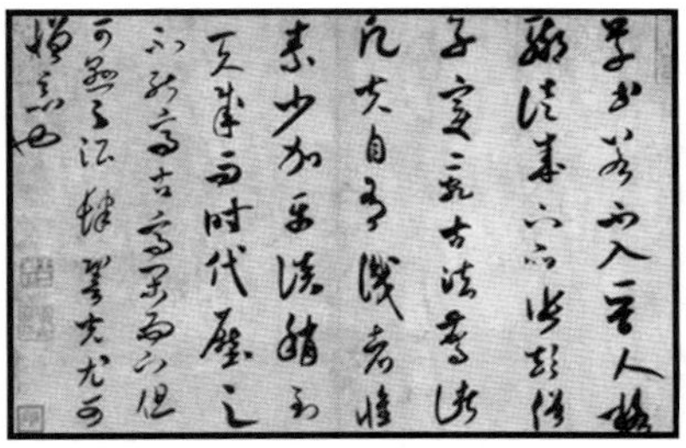

Mifu's Chinese calligraphy
Sang Dynasty

Let's consider pattern and arrangement of shapes on flat surfaces. We will not attempt to create the illusion of depth; only the arrangement of lines and shapes within a frame will be examined. In short, let's evaluate the **visual composition** of pictures, paintings, prints, and other "flat" works of art.

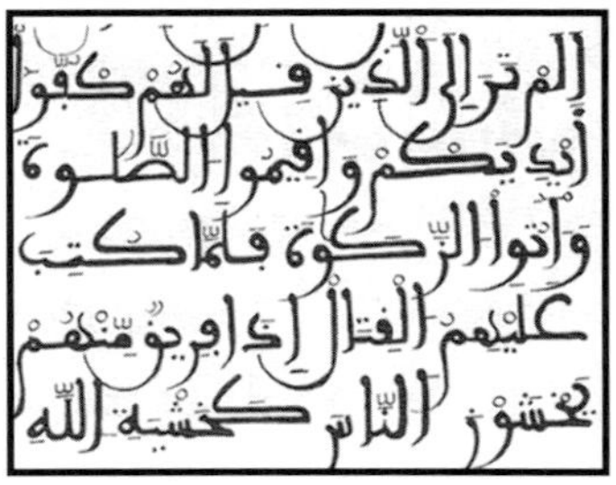

Islamic calligraphy
Andalus Quran

Name: Date:

Producing Two-dimensional Works of Art

Answer the questions below to test your knowledge of two-dimensional art.

1. Which dimensions does a two-dimensional work of art have?

   (A) width and length

   (B) length and depth

   (C) depth and width

2. A two-dimensional piece of art appears ______ .

   (A) colourful

   (B) sunken

   (C) flat

3. "Flat" works of art are considered as ______ .

   (A) unattractive, boring, and uncreative

   (B) design, pattern, or decoration

   (C) life like, full of depth and value

4. What is visual composition?

   (A) the placement and arrangement of lines and shapes in a work of art

   (B) the object you see in a picture

   (C) the scale of a work

Name: Date:

Producing Two-dimensional Works of Art

A. Which of the following are representations of two-dimensional images? Write "2D" in the circles of the images that are and "X" in those that are not.

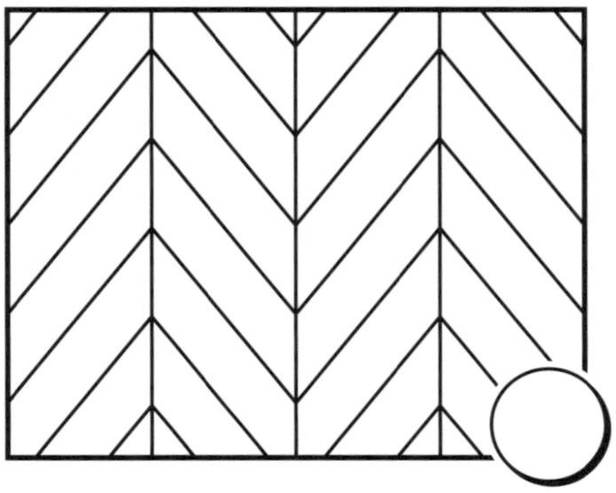

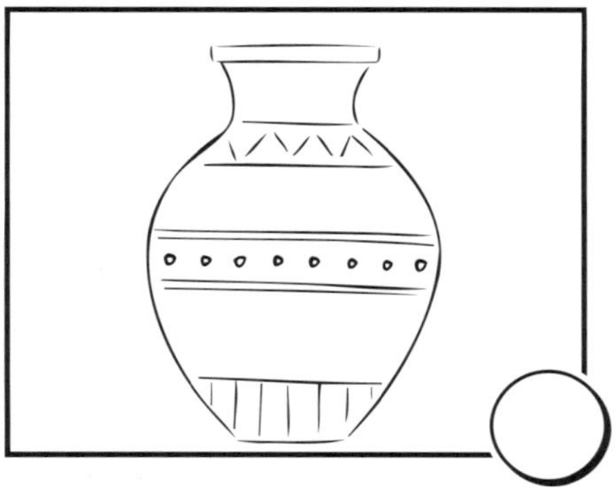
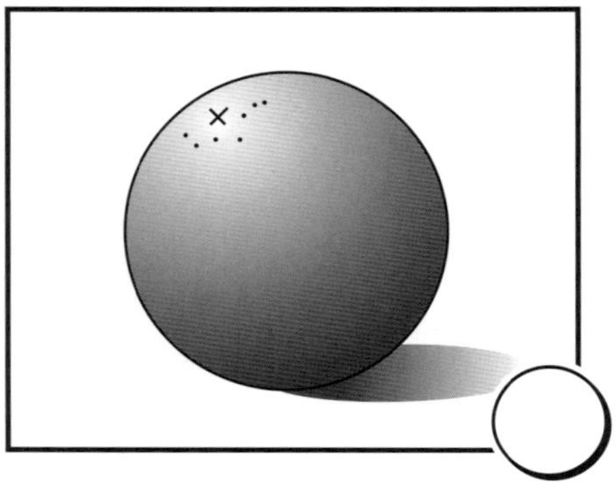
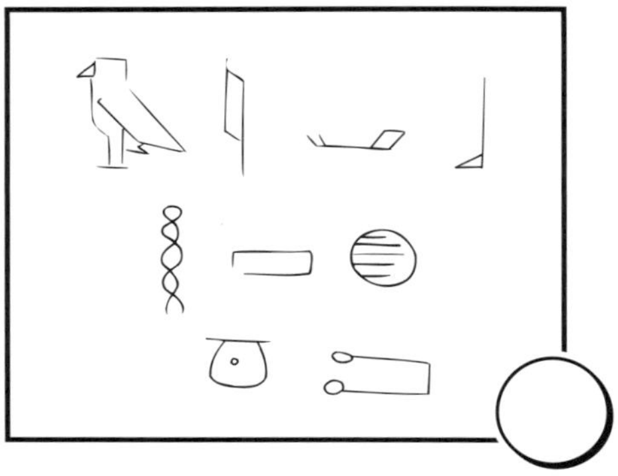

B. Create a two-dimensional piece of art in the space provided.

Name: Date:

Producing Two-dimensional Works of Art

Motivation:

To recognize and produce good design limited to two-dimensions and to make a pleasing design using shapes which are drawn or cut out of paper and magazines

Materials:

- pencil, paper, ruler, and compass
- 16 x 20" Bristol board, coloured or white
- scissors and glue stick

What to Do:

1 Make a graphic design (arrangement of shapes) using one of the three options below:

letters / numbers / shapes (from nature, like oak leaves or starfish)

2 Cut out all of the shapes (letters, numbers, shapes, etc.) to be arranged in your final artwork. These shapes do not have to be in their usual positions – you might turn them sideways or even upside-down! Use different sizes as well as colours.

3 Experiment with how you would like to arrange the shapes on the Bristol board. Make an interesting composition by having the shapes touch one another.

4 Design a plan for the arrangement of the 2-D design elements as a rough draft. Use one design pattern for the background of the picture and another to fill in the themed silhouette. Your rough draft can be smaller than the final but it is best to do the same size.

5 Draw or glue your shapes onto your choice of Bristol board.

Name: Date:

Producing Three-dimensional Art

Objective: *To produce two- and three-dimensional works of art that communicate a range of thoughts, feelings, and ideas for specific purposes and to specific audiences*

Three-dimensional works of art are all around us.

Did you ever think of yourself as a three-dimensional work of art?

Have you ever seen a human or animal turned to stone as animated in the movie The Chronicles of Narnia?

Pieta
Michelangelo, 1499

Artists throughout the ages have tried to sculpt the human figure as a permanent object. One of the earliest caveman artifacts found by archaeologists in Europe was a sculpture of the Venus of Willendorf, made about 12 000 BCE or 15 000 years ago. It is a simple stone carving of a female figure.

All cultures in the past and up to the present have carved, cast, or sculpted the human figure for many different reasons. These figures, even though thousands of years old, are often in near perfect condition! They are usually found in museums or private art collections. Because they were made of very durable materials like stone, copper, bronze, or steel, they withstood the passing of time.

When you go to an art museum, you will probably find many big sculptures more than ten feet high, or small statutes in glass cases. These sculptures may be made of stone such as marble or metals like bronze or gold.

One of the things you will quickly discover is that creating these figures is harder than it looks. Making a reasonable looking figure of an animal or human being is not a simple thing to do. Just like hockey players and figure skaters make their sports seem easy, you may find that sculpting three-dimensional art seems easy to do too.

Name: Date:

Producing Three-dimensional Art

Find three examples of sculptures in magazines or around you. Paste or draw pictures of them in the circles. Then describe the shape of each sculpture, the material it is made of, and where it is displayed.

1.

Figure: ______________________

Material: ______________________

Location: ______________________

2.

Figure: ______________________

Material: ______________________

Location: ______________________

3.

Figure: ______________________

Material: ______________________

Location: ______________________

Name: Date:

Producing Three-dimensional Art

Look at these three-dimensional figures. Circle the material most commonly used to create their three-dimensional forms.

1. Figurine

marble **wax**

porcelain

2. Action Figure

wood **plastic**

stone

3. Garden Gnome

paper **stone**

sand

4. Model Ship

paper **wood** **glass**

5. Water Fountain

stone **plastic**

wood

6. Origami

paper **plastic** **stone**

Name: Date:

Producing Three-dimensional Art

Motivation:

To create a three-dimensional sculpture or model out of a bar of soap

Materials:

- pencils
- soft bar of soap
- plastic knife
- plastic fork
- toothpicks

What to Do:

1. Line your work area with newspaper to catch the soap that is scraped from the bar.

2. Using a pencil, make the outline of your figure or design on the soap.

3. Use a plastic knife to scrape off small sections of the bar, whittling it into your desired figure or design.

4. When you have scraped your bar into a form that is similar to the figure or design you want, use the toothpick or fork to create the details. Use different techniques and pressures to make interesting grooves into the soap.

   *Caution: do not press too hard or the soap will break.

5. Once you have completed the soap sculpture, store it in a cool dry place where people can admire your work!

Remember to hold your soap gently, making sure not to hold it too tight, or else you could crush or soften it.

Name: Date:

Strengths and Improvements in Art

Objective: *To identify strengths and areas of improvement in your work and in that of others*

What would you say if your friend asked your opinion on her art?

Would you take a quick look and tell her, "It's great," or would you offer some helpful and thoughtful comments?

A person who reviews art is called an art critic. There are different critics for all types of art and they all have extensive training in each of their individual fields. They evaluate a work of art based on different factors, and then they write a *critique* (pronounced kri-teek) – an essay about its strengths and limitations.

In real life, everyone is a critic. Everyone has his or her own likes and dislikes and individual reasons for them. However, critiquing art is about so much more than personal taste; in fact, personal likes and dislikes have nothing to do with it!

When evaluating art, critics look for strengths and weaknesses within the work of art. To figure out those strengths and weaknesses, they consider different things. They take into account style, technique, composition (how it's put together), colour, theme, and the message of the piece. But that does not even scratch the surface of what critics think about. They also take into context when, where, and by whom it was made; whether it was a man or woman, the artist's nationality, and the list goes on and on.

This project will require you to be a critic of your own artwork and perhaps of works by others in your class. You will write *critiques* of the artwork you've made this past year and perhaps some of your classmates' works. Keep in mind that this project is all about finding strengths in art and suggesting ways of improving it, not about your personal opinion.

Name: Date:

Strengths and Improvements in Art

For each kind of art, give four factors you might consider when evaluating or critiqing that piece.

Factors to be considered

size colour movement style texture material weather structure

Painting

Sculpture

Dance (Ballet)

Architecture

Name: Date:

Strengths and Improvements in Art

Note the materials that the children used to create their artwork. Think of two strengths for each piece and give two suggestions for improvement.

1. *I used wire to form the body. Then I pressed clay onto and around the wire body, making arms and legs. I used a toothpick to carve out the features.*

____

____

____

____

____

____

2. *I used half of a walnut to make the head. Then I glued googly eyes, a corn kernel, seeds, and yarn to the head making a face. I also twisted a thin wire into glasses.*

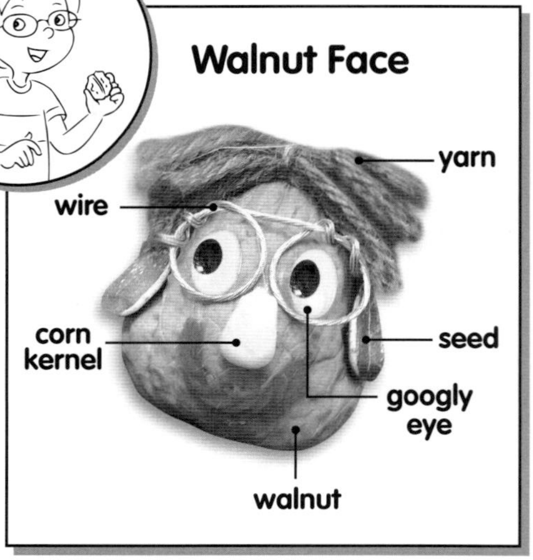

____

____

____

____

____

____

____

Name: Date:

Strengths and Improvements in Art

Motivation:

To write and evaluate the strengths and areas of improvement in students' art from the past year, and to form your own opinion about a work of art and compare it to another's

Materials:

- pen
- paper

What to Do:

Find a review of a movie you have seen from a newspaper or magazine. Cut it out and paste it to the page. Then say whether or not you agree with the review and why.

Movie Review

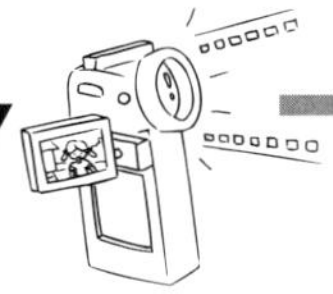

My Review ____________________

____

____

____

Next, review all your works of art from this past year. Choose one of them and write about its strengths and areas in need of improvement.

Name: Date:

Popular Art Themes

Objective: *To compare works on a similar theme*

Napoleon
Jean-Baptiste Isabey

Have you ever read a book that has been made into a movie? Most movies and some TV shows start out as novels. Some good examples of this are: Little House on the Prairie, Lord of the Rings, and The Chronicles of Narnia.

Napoleon
Jacques-Louis David

These are all examples of works of art on a similar theme. Authors use words, and sometimes sketches or pictures to tell stories, whereas filmmakers use actors, places, and sometimes animation to create stories.

Artists have been recording and capturing the same themes, topics, events, and important occasions throughout history. Time and time again, great leaders have been the subjects of portraits, sculptures, and murals. The pharaohs of Egypt, Jesus of Nazareth, Alexander the Great, Napoleon, and Abraham Lincoln are all famous people who have been painted and sculpted by different artists over the ages. However, the works of art portraying these people do not all look the same. The artists might have created works on a similar theme, but the end results were unique.

Another common subject used repeatedly in art is the "Mother and Child" portrait. This subject has been a favourite theme of artists for thousands of years. Identifying popular themes in art allows us to make comparisons between art periods and artists. It can also help us identify different artistic techniques and evaluate the uniqueness of a work of art.

The Crucifixion
Mathis Gothart Grunewald

Cristo crucificdo
Velzquez, Diego

Name: Date:

Popular Art Themes

Give examples of two popular cartoon characters of the variety indicated. Draw or paste a picture of each character. List three similarities they have.

Princesses

Their Similarities

Superheroes

Their Similarities

Name: Date:

Popular Art Themes

Read what each child says. Then identify which popular theme is the subject of the painting in question. Choose your answer from the list provided and write it on the line.

Religion Still Life Romance Animals Portrait War

A likeness of a person, either famous or not, living or dead. Focus is mainly on the face and expressions.

____

Inanimate objects are the centre of attention. It could be a bowl of fruit or vase filled with flowers.

____

Spiritual inspiration drives artists to create images of angels, churches, holy artifacts, or sacred events.

____

The mystery and love of wildlife moves artists to capture all sorts of beasts in paintings.

____

Name: Date:

Popular Art Themes

Materials:

- pencils, paper, ruler
- Bristol board (white and coloured)
- various materials such as cloth, pasta, and rice
- poster paints, brushes, ink, markers, and crayons
- white glue and glue stick

Motivation:

To make art on a similar theme using two different techniques and colour schemes and to consider and produce art with the same image in two different ways

What to Do:

1. Choose a theme and subject matter, for example, sea creatures or flowers in a garden.
2. Make a rough draft (preliminary drawing) of your image.
3. Transfer your outline image to two different 6 x 8" pieces of white and/or coloured Bristol board.
4. One at a time, create the same image with two completely different sets of materials. For example, make one with noodles and beans and the other in complete detail with paint and coloured ink.
5. Make a Bristol board matt (frame) for each of the images; the best would be one matt with two openings side by side with your art taped to the back.

Name: Date:

Art in Different Periods or Cultures

Objective: *To compare works on a similar theme from various periods and cultures, and to describe the impact of time and location on a work of art*

Do you skate or read the same way now as you did when you were five years old? Most likely you do not. Skill and ability improve with every year of practice and study that passes.

The visual arts record the advancement and/or regression in humanity's ability to portray ideas, emotions, and messages. By doing this, visual art acts as a timeline, illustrating the different styles, functions, and favoured themes of different historical periods. The visual arts can also show differences between historical periods through each generation's interpretation of a similar theme. For example, a medieval rendition of Christ's crucifixion is very different from a Victorian interpretation.

Art can be a visual message not only from another time but also from another place. It allows us to tell apart historical periods and different cultures. If you compare two landscape paintings, one of Canada by a Canadian artist, and another of China by a Chinese artist, you would most likely be able to tell them apart quite easily. This would be because of the differences in not only the countries' landscapes but also their cultures. Through visual arts, we have the opportunity to distinguish between different cultures and historical periods – a valuable asset to humankind.

Different Periods
(Pottery of ancient Greece)

Bilingual amphora,
520 BCE

Proto-Corinthian olpe,
640-30 BCE

Different Cultures

The Circus
Georges Seurat, 1891

Magnolia and Erect Rock
Chen Hongshou, 1598-1652

Name: Date:

Art in Different Periods or Cultures

Say whether each is an advancement or regression in artistry. Write either "advancement" or "regression" on the given line.

1.

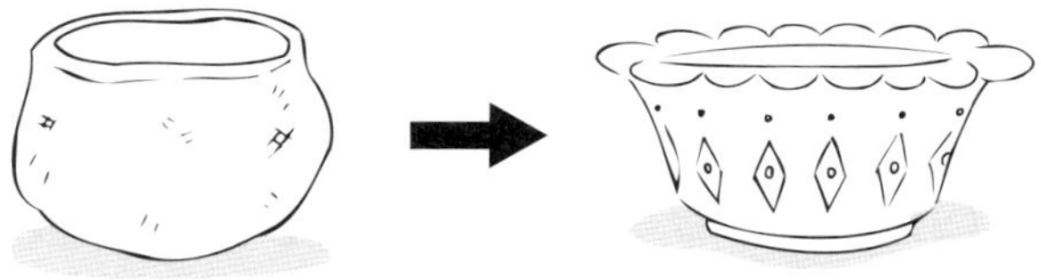

____

2.

____

3.

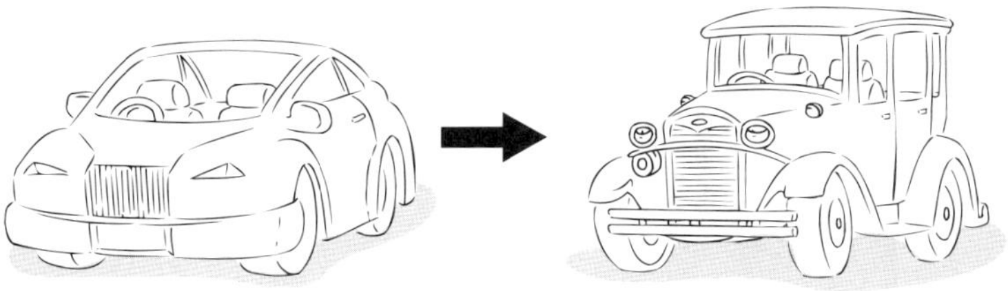

____

4.

____

5.

____

Name: Date:

Art in Different Periods or Cultures

Identify the art period for each piece of artwork. Then match the descriptions to their correct art periods.

art period

- **Renaissance**
- **Baroque**
- **Modern Art**
- **Post-modern Art**

description

- ***extremely detail-oriented***
- ***heavily favoured abstraction***
- ***uses technology, particularly video and collage***
- ***human-centred and displays the beauty of nature***

1.

The Scream
Edvard Munch

M ________________ A __________ ;

____

2.

Still-life
Josefa de Óbidos

B ________________ ;

____

3.

The Sistine Madonna
Raphael

R ________________ ;

____

4.

Cut with the Dada Kitchen Knife through the Last Weimar Beer-Belly Cultural Epoch in Germany
Hannah Höch

P ________________ A __________ ;

____

Name: Date:

Art in Different Periods or Cultures

Motivation:

To produce a piece of pottery from a specified culture and time

Materials:

- paper and pencils for basic design work
- Crayola Model Magic or similar product (dry hard modelling clay)
- poster paints, coloured markers, India ink, and brushes

What to Do:

Day 1

1. Choose a period or culture – e.g. Medieval, Renaissance, Modern, Asian, African, or European.
2. Research the time period and place of your choice. This requires library or computer lab time to look up information for your project.
3. Draw some preliminary designs of the shape, form, and decoration of your pottery.

Day 2

4. Form the pot out of the modelling clay.
5. Allow it to dry and harden.
6. Then decorate with paints, inks, or markers for an authentic look.

Present the finished products and compare them with your classmates!

Name: Date:

Lines that Direct Attention

Objective: *To describe how lines can be used to direct the viewer's attention*

When directing someone who is lost, we often point them in the direction they need to go. In most cases, we use our hands and arms to form a line, directing their path. Imagine trying to give directions without doing this – using statements like "Over there!" or "Right beside that thing!" without the help of that line!

In art, the focus point is the destination, and the lines used to direct the viewer's attention to the focus point are like the line you make with your arm when guiding someone who is lost. In both cases, without influencing the viewer's gaze, they might not know where or what to look at. Not having these lines would be confusing and frustrating for both the director and the lost person, or in the art world, the artist and the art viewer.

The composition of lines in a piece of art is just as important and has just as much of an effect as the types of lines used. For instance, diverting attention from images in the foreground can be achieved by using straight, vertical lines that lead to images in the middle or backgrounds. Also, drawing many straight, diagonal lines that meet at the same image would make that image stand out against other images in a painting. Lines can be used not only to attract attention but to distract it as well. Using many wavy or curvy lines that run opposite the main image in a painting would draw focus away from the image.

Our attention is directed by lines every day, not just in works of art. Next time you are buttoning your shirt, notice how the seam guides your attention from the top button to the bottom one, or vice versa. And, when you see a cathedral, take a moment to notice the lines of the tower; they will most likely be guiding your attention to a cross at its peak.

Name: Date:

Lines that Direct Attention

Modify the focus point of the picture on the right with the use of lines. Then compare the picture on the left to the picture on the right. Do the lines you've created draw your attention to or away from the specified point?

Move Focus Away from Foreground

Distract Focus from the Fruit

Choose One Point of Focus

Name: Date:

Lines that Direct Attention

Complete the picture by finding the direction your attention is being drawn to, and drawing something at the focus point.

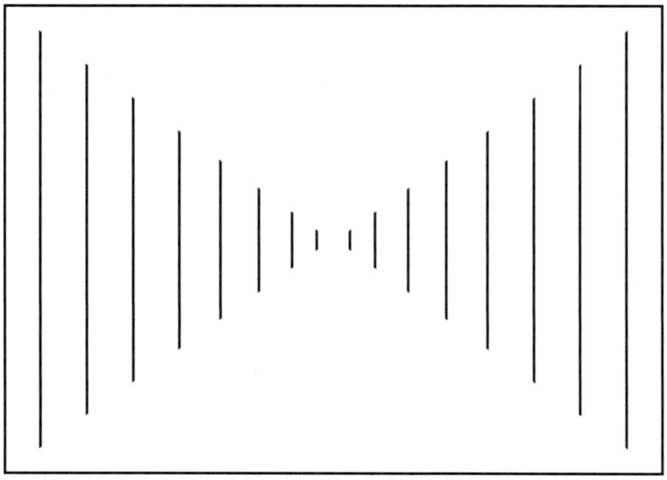

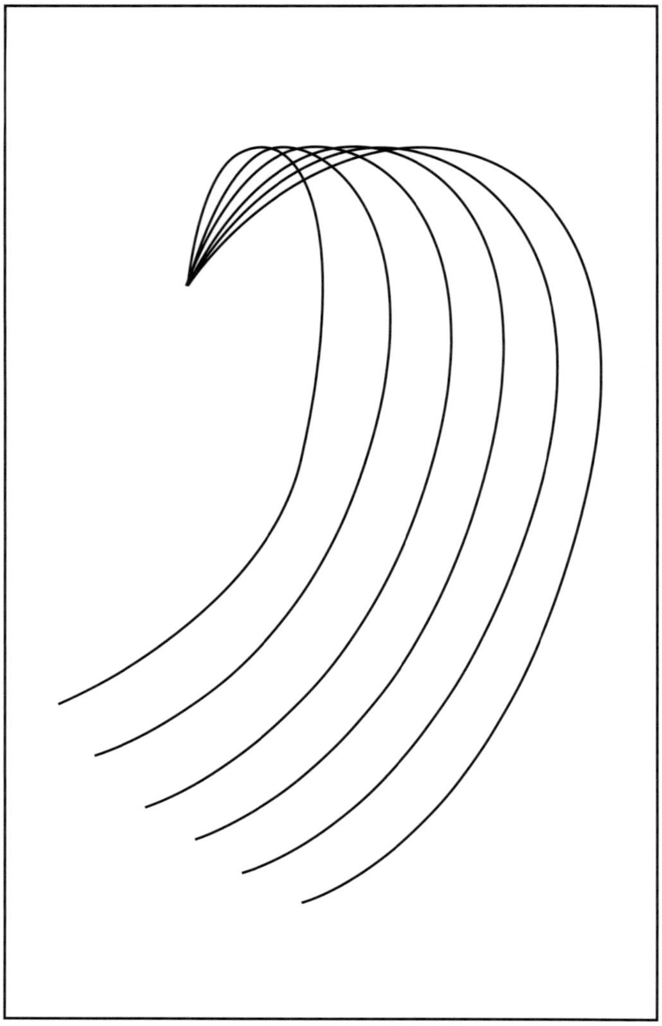

Name: Date:

Lines that Direct Attention

Materials:

- 11 x 14" coloured or white paper and pencil
- large colour or black and white photograph of a street scene from a magazine
- glue stick
- red coloured pencils, wax crayons, or felt pens
- ruler and compass or 2 pencils held together with rubber bands

Motivation:

To make an art project using lines to direct the viewer's attention as intended by the student

What to Do:

1. Cut out the photograph of your choice.
2. Glue it onto the middle of your larger sheet of white paper to create a frame.
3. Study the picture for lines, for instance along a wall, fence, or roadway.
4. Draw red lines along these "hidden lines" to show exactly where they are and to what point they lead (the vanishing point).
5. Display all the results as a large mural for all to see.

The Agony in the Garden
Andrea Mantegna

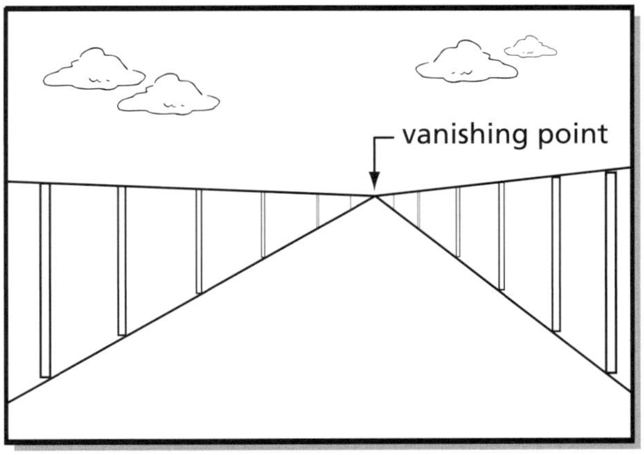

Name: Date:

The Function of Art in the Community

Objective: *To identify the function of visual art in your community and the contribution that it makes to the economy*

Have you ever seen a large sculpture in a park or outside a building?

Have you ever read a poem written on a wall or displayed in the subway?

Why do you think this is done? What would the function of such pieces be? Do you think you would stop to look at them? Maybe you would even take a moment to talk about them with your friends. If this is what you would do, then the pieces of art have served a function. They have brought people together in discussion.

Art is often a way of creating beauty. Transforming a dreary and sad space into a more aesthetically-pleasing one could have many effects. It could not only brighten our mood when we see it, but also create a sense of togetherness. The idea that people of a community can come together to create art with the intention that it will give pleasure to others can inspire fellowship and increase everyone's quality of life.

Lastly, why are beautifully-crafted statues and sculptures installed outside buildings and in parks? In this case, there is a specific purpose for erecting these pieces in outdoor, public spaces; the intention is not solely to beautify a space. Many of these monuments commemorate an event. Their locations are chosen according to relevance, importance, and popularity. Despite its location, the function of the piece remains the same, that is, to remind people of a specific person or event.

The functions of art in a community are unlimited and are most often positive. Art is being installed in new communities every day with the hope of improving people's lives.

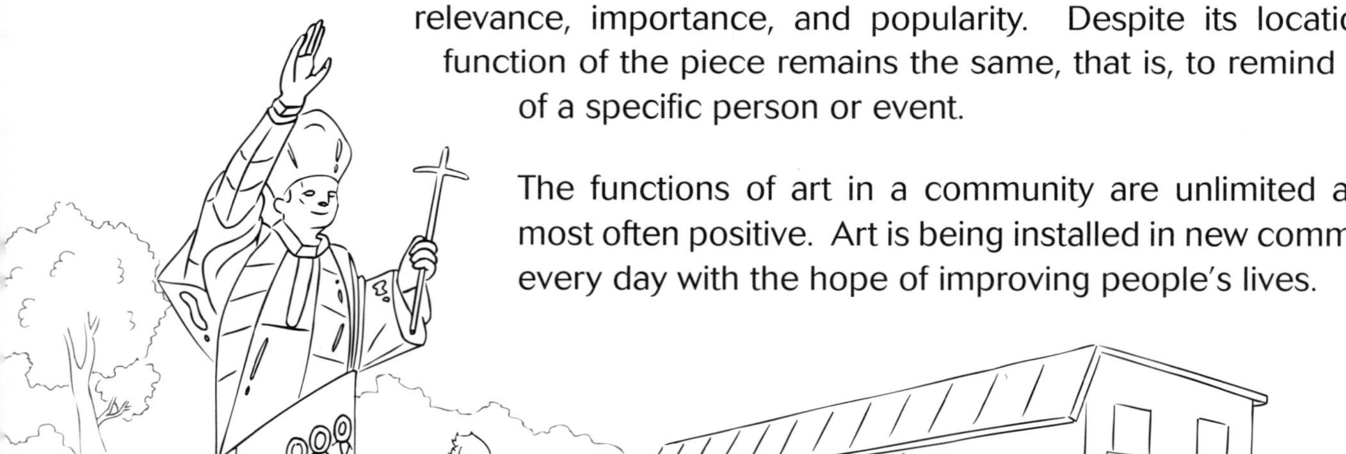

Name: Date:

The Function of Art in the Community

A. Give a reason why you think poetry would appear on a bus, subway, or street car.

B. Design a mural to be put in your community. Draw your idea for a mural on the building wall below.

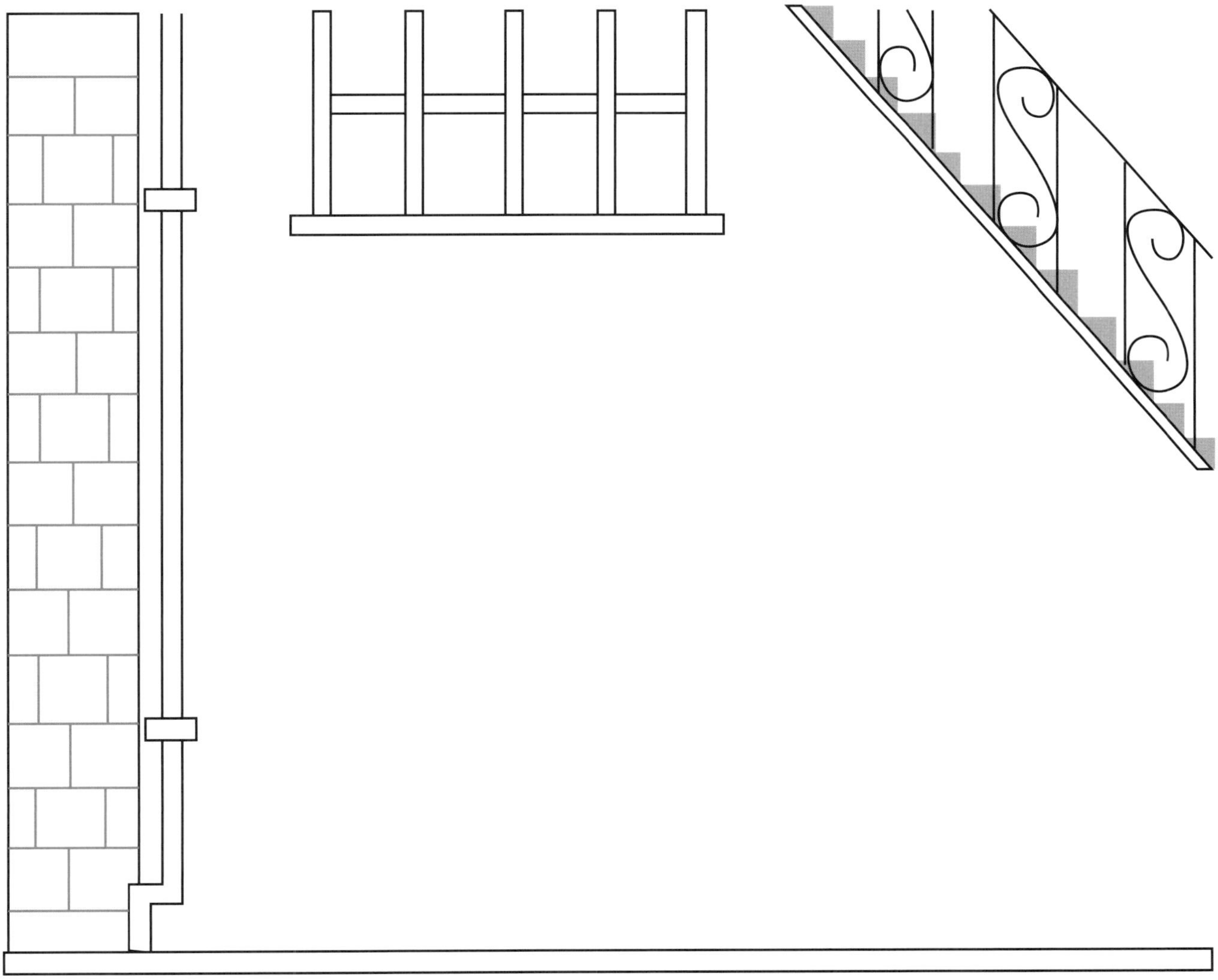

Name: Date:

The Function of Art in the Community

Think of a space in your community that you think needs a piece of art. Write what kind of art you would put there, where the location is, and what its function would be. Then draw a sketch of the work in its location in the space provided.

Artwork for My Community

Location: ____________________

Artwork: ____________________

Function: ____________________

____

Name: Date:

The Function of Art in the Community

Materials:

- paper, coloured pencils, ruler, and compass for rough draft and final work
- 16 x 20″ white or coloured Bristol board or poster board
- poster paint and brushes, coloured paper, inks, markers
- special materials: aluminum foil, felt, ribbon or – be creative with what you include

Motivation:

To recognize, appreciate, and produce a work of art with a function in the community and to make an advertisement for a cause

What to Do:

1 Start at the beginning, and answer these questions to make a TO-DO list:

- What is the main topic, good cause, or organization?
- Who is the target group? (the main group you want to reach)
- What images or designs should be in the poster?
- What information is needed by the target group?
- What letter style and size is best for the purpose?
- What is the mood of the poster? (Is it fun, serious, inviting, or informing?)
- What style or compilation is best for the purpose of the poster?
- What things can you do to really attract attention to your cause?

2 Make the final poster by enlarging your best rough draft after it has been teacher approved.

Put together ideas using the answers to these questions. Make sketches to figure out what works and what would look best. Look, this is my poster!

Name: Date:

Creating Movement and Depth with Lines

Objective: *To identify how lines may be used to create movement and depth*

Escaping Criticism
Pere Borrell del Caso, 1874

There are many works of art that give the illusion of depth and movement in their composition. Creating the illusion of depth and movement is like a magic trick. Artists trick art observers by creating the sense that images are moving out of or disappearing into the background of their pictures.

As with all magic tricks, special knowledge and technique is involved in their production. Consider the art technique used to "trick the eye", Trompe l'oeil; its extremely realistic optical illusions are like nothing else! The realistic images produced by this art technique are created with the use of lines that give images depth that are incredibly life like. See how the child in Caso's piece, *Escaping Criticism,* is literally jumping out of the picture!

Illusions of movement and depth can also be seen in sculpted works. Sculptors use very precise combinations of lines when chiselling away at their chosen material. These combinations of lines create not only the illusion of depth but actual depth as well.

The endless ways to compile lines allows for unlimited kinds of movement to be portrayed. The sculpture, *Pluto and Proserpina,* by Gian Bernini shows at least three different movements at once, all created with the use of lines: Proserpina's hair blowing in the wind, Pluto holding on tight to Proserpina, and the three-headed dog (Hades) barking. This piece is a perfect example of the movement and depth that can be created with lines.

Name: Date:

Creating Movement and Depth with Lines

Use the types of lines indicated to create movement.

Lava Exploding (heavy, straight lines)

Heat Rising (light, broken, wavy lines)

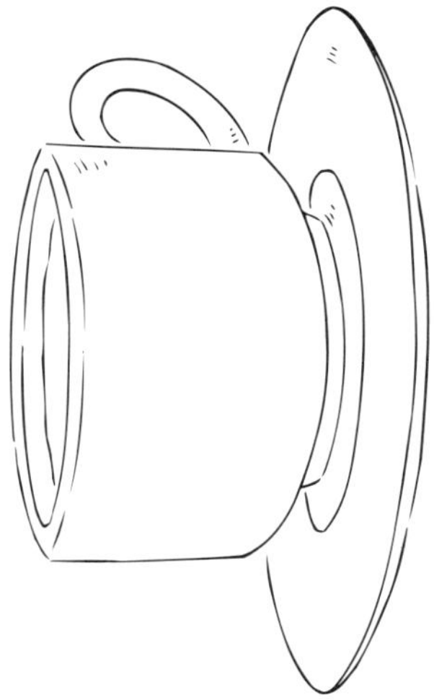

Waves Crashing (sharp, curvy lines)

Shivering (short, vertical, wavy lines)

Name: Date:

Creating Movement and Depth with Lines

Trace the dotted lines to experience how depth is created. Then add shading to make depth more pronounced.

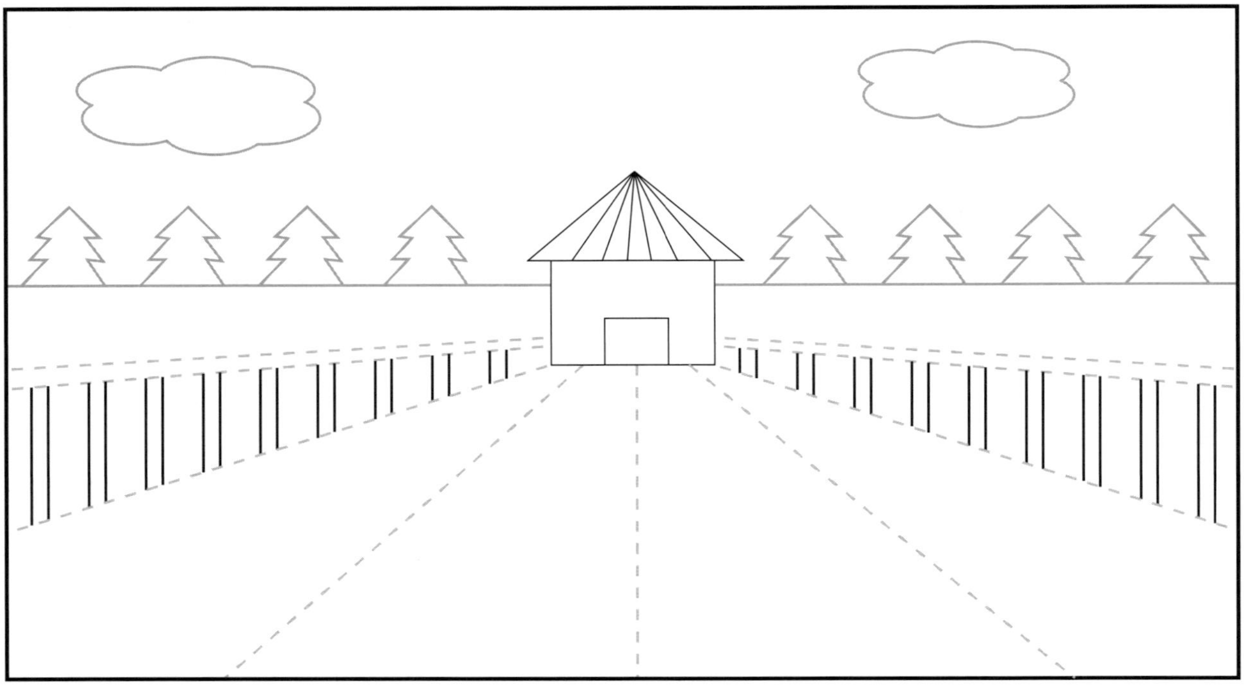

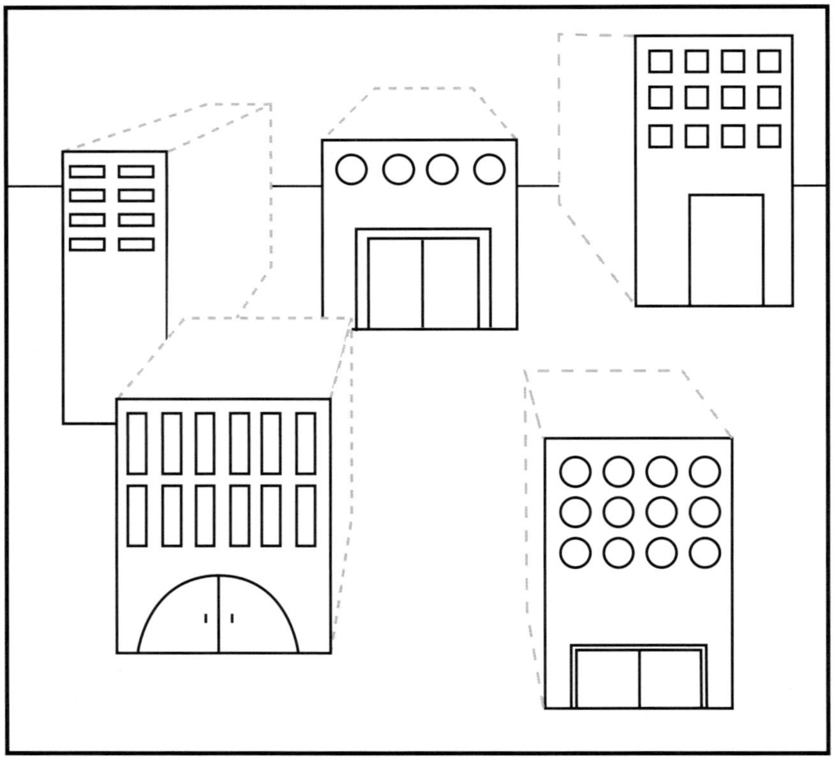

Name: Date:

Creating Movement and Depth with Lines

Materials:

- 8.5 x 11" white paper for pencil work, Bristol board for paint work
- ruler
- coloured pencils held together with rubber bands
- coloured poster paints or coloured inks
- shaped sponges (hearts, stars, moons, etc.)

Motivation:

To show an understanding of simple techniques used to create the illusion of depth and movement in art

What to Do:

Activity 1: Creating Movement

1. Use pencils held together, 2 or 3 at a time, to make large sweeping lines on the page.
2. Change colours to make your work more interesting with combinations of curves, waves, and zigzag lines. All of these will help give the impression of movement in your picture.
3. Use a little paint on a sponge, but not too much, to draw at least 3 lines out to all edges of the page from the spot you've picked on the blank Bristol board.

Activity 2: Creating Depth

1. Pick a spot on a blank Bristol board and use your ruler to draw at least 12 lines out to the edges.
2. Colour the spaces reaching out to the corners of the page in pairs with 2 different colours leaving the space in-between blank.
3. Draw a third line on either side of each of the coloured areas and fill it with black. You have now created the illusion of depth with beams made by lines!

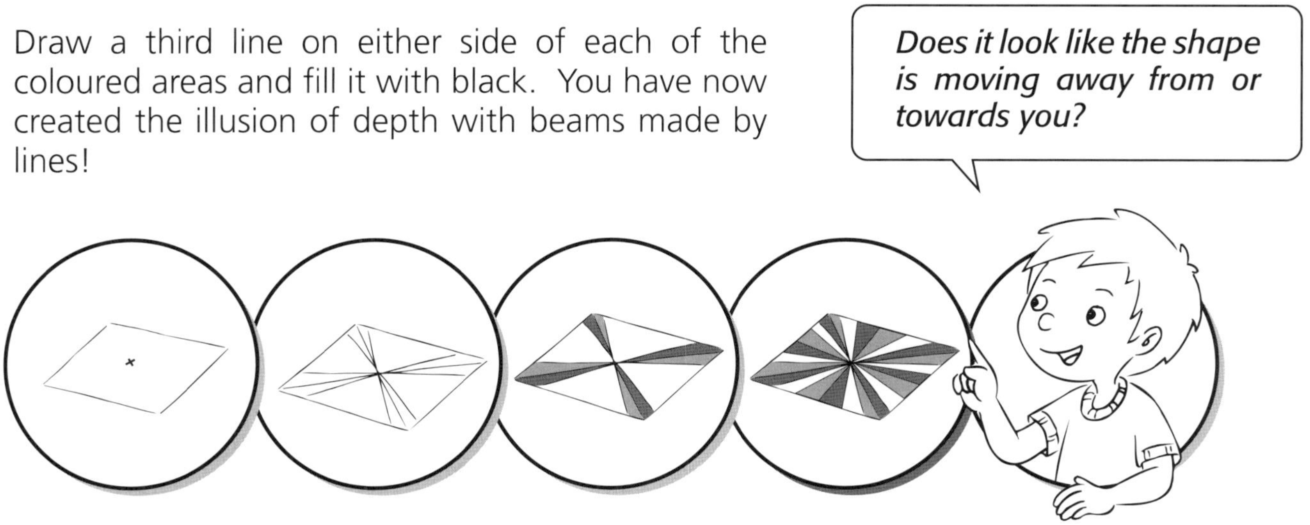

Name: Date:

Defining Shapes and Forms with Lines

Objective: *To describe how lines may be used to define shapes and forms*

Cave wall
Lascaux, France

Some of the earliest man-made shapes and forms on Earth can be found on cave walls in Lascaux, France. These images were created by primitive tribes as much as 10 to 15 thousand years ago. These paintings of animal figures can be seen as some of the earliest visual aids for art education.

The images found in those caves were often made with primitive tools and materials such as charcoal on the end of a burnt stick and paint made from minerals available in that region. They suggest that the earliest method of making a line was to drag a stick across the ground.

The manipulation of lines to create images has evolved considerably since the days of cave painting. However, some features remain the same; the lines used to create two-dimensional shapes are still quite similar, yet putting lines together to create forms has evolved greatly. Today, creating the illusion of depth has improved significantly, allowing artists to create forms in different sizes and figures.

Shapes
(height and width)

Forms
(height, width, depth)

The definition of shapes and forms is part of a system of design called "geometry", by the Greek. Geometry is the science of using lines to draw **shape** – two dimensions (height and width) and **form** – three dimensions (height, width, and depth). These two basic aspects of design, shape and form, are often confused or interchanged, even by adults. This lesson should help set the record straight.

Name: Date:

Defining Shapes and Forms with Lines

A. Consider the following and indicate whether you would be seeing a shape (two dimensions) or a form (three dimensions). Write "shape" or "form" on the line.

1. Looking at a flat photograph ____________
2. Watching a three-dimensional movie ____________
3. Looking at a relief sculpture ____________
4. Watching TV on a flat screen ____________

B. Draw the same geometrical figure in both boxes. Then add the illusion of depth to one of the shapes using shading or overlapping to make it a form.

Name: Date:

Defining Shapes and Forms with Lines

Choose a shape (star, triangle, circle, etc.). Then find images of different forms of the same colour in old magazines. Arrange the cutouts into the shape you have chosen. Glue them in place in the box below.

Defining Shapes and Forms with Lines

Motivation:

To make a collage using a variety of shapes

Materials:

- 8.5 x 11″ white or coloured paper
- pencil, ruler, compass
- coloured pencils
- markers
- scissors and glue stick
- magazine photos
- newspaper

What to Do:

1 Using pencil, coloured pencils, or cut out pieces of coloured paper, make a pattern with different-sized geometric shapes: squares, circles, triangles, rectangles, and polygons – use overlapping.

2 Using cut-out photographs from magazines, make a collage with pictures of all the basic forms: cubes and boxes, things that are cylinders, etc.

Name: Date:

Identifying Negative and Positive Shapes

Objective: *To identify negative and positive shapes in works of art and the environment*

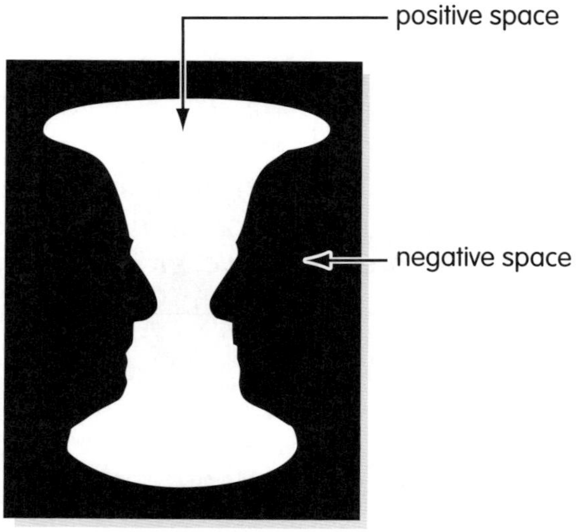

Negative shapes are something you have been looking at for years and might not have even noticed them. You have probably never even considered negative shapes, unlike positive shapes, which you discovered at a very early age. Think about the area around and between objects and forms. These spaces are always there, but we don't normally notice them. We are always asked about the forms we do see (positive shapes) and seldom about those we do not see (negative shapes).

Take a second look at the objects around you and try to make images of the negative spaces around them. Draw your attention to what you almost never look at; consider the space around what you usually look at, and what confines it. Artists throughout history have been aware of and have used negative space as part of their works.

The first step in this lesson is to change the way we think and see. This may be a bit difficult at first. Try not to get discouraged if it takes you a little while. Once you shift your way of viewing things, it's all very simple. Just look around at what you have been overlooking. One way to do this is to look at a space as though it were on a TV screen or within a picture frame. Start to border off an area of view to make it easier to spot those negative spaces. Look at the space between the concrete objects that are within the frame. Then, try to identify the forms of those negative spaces; do you see a triangle, a square, or a circle?

Name: Date:

Identifying Negative and Positive Shapes

Colour the pictures below following the given instructions. Then identify the positive and negative shapes.

1.

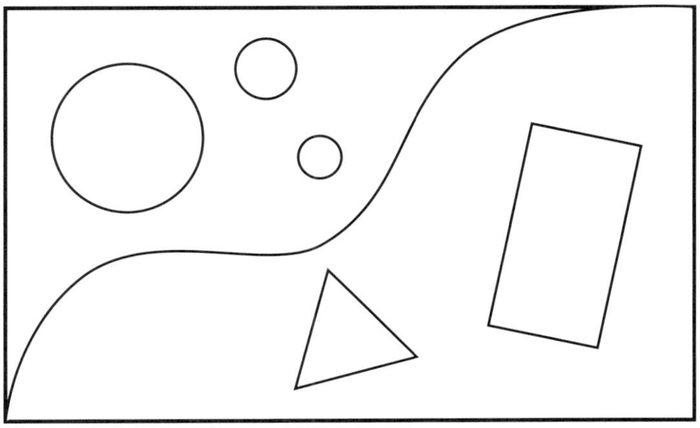

Instructions:

- Colour the circles black.
- Colour the part under the wavy line black except the triangle and rectangle.

Negative Shapes: ______________________

Positive Shapes: ______________________

2.

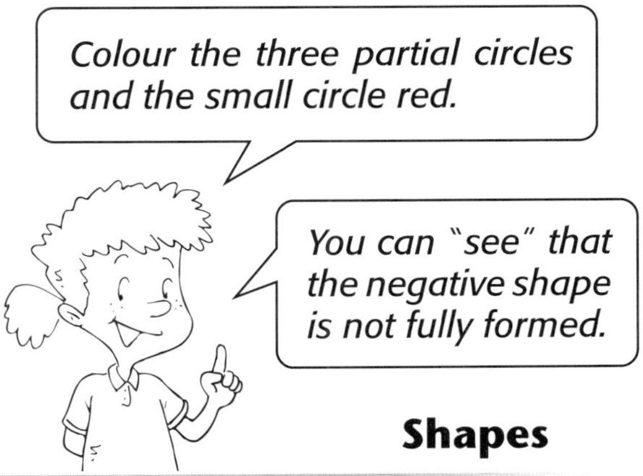

Shapes
Negative
Positive

Name: Date:

Identifying Negative and Positive Shapes

Find the following negative shapes in magazines or newspapers. Cut them out and glue them in the box below. Then highlight the negative shapes in the images to make them stand out.

Negative Shapes

Name: Date:

Identifying Negative and Positive Shapes

Materials:

- markers
- paper
- scissors
- pencil
- ruler
- black construction paper
- glue stick

Motivation:

To identify and draw negative space in an art project

What to Do:

1 Take your paper and pencil and draw an object that has both negative and positive spaces. (a chair, a desk, etc.) Draw the image the length and width of the page, leaving a 1.5" margin on all sides.

2 Cut out all of the positive shapes leaving nothing but the negative space. Do not lose any of the negative space pieces that might have been cut out as a result.

3 Glue the white paper with the positive shape(s) onto the black paper.

4 Observe the image left by the negative space. Notice how negative space can be just as distinct as the positive space.

e.g.

Draw a chair.

Cut out the chair and all remaining negative spaces.

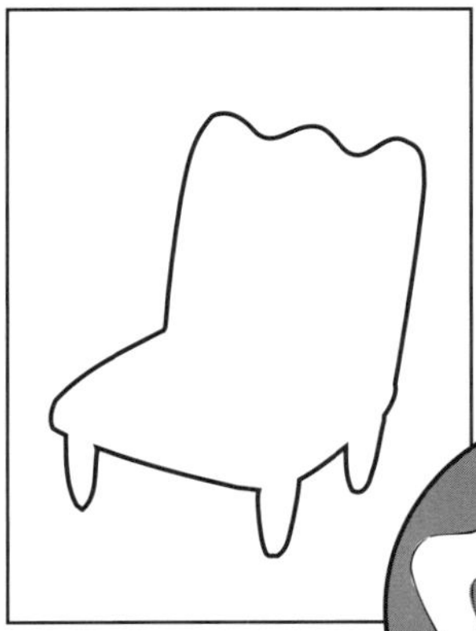

Name: Date:

Creating Depth with Shading

Objective: *To identify how the shading of shapes can be used to create the illusion of depth*

If you see a sculpture in a museum, you might notice that a spotlight is shining on it. It reveals the beautiful shadows of its form, showcasing its three-dimensional qualities.

How does light appear when a spotlight is placed on still life objects as opposed to when it is taken away? How do we get the viewer to believe they are seeing that which is not really there on a flat page? What are the differences in the shapes of the shaded areas?

The answer lies in the ability to create a kind of illusion. Shading is a method of creating the illusion of depth in art; it is what the artists of the Italian Renaissance called *chiaroscuro*, "light and dark".

In everyday experience, light does not bend; it shines in a straight line. Because light cannot bend around corners, it does not light objects up evenly or all the way around them. The simple result is that some parts of objects in still life, as we observe them, are not "lit up". In other words, they are "in the dark". Dark is commonly referred to as "shade" and explains how we are creating the illusion of depth using shading.

Learning to apply "shading" correctly is the key to making this illusion work. Effectively using the source of light, the sun or a light bulb, is the first part of our understanding. The second part is a single object, for example a ball, and how light is cast on it. Because light does not bend, the side of the ball on the opposite side of the light source is shaded or darker. The amount of shade increases (gradation), as you go around to the side farthest from the source of light. The darkest shading on a curved form is the edge opposite the source of the light.

Name: Date:

Creating Depth with Shading

Circle the correct answers. Then cut out the pictures and glue them to the matching descriptions in the questions.

1. Shading
   A. creates the illusion of depth.
   B. is light.

2. Light
   A. can bend.
   B. moves in a straight line.

3. A shading technique includes
   A. hatching.
   B. scratching.

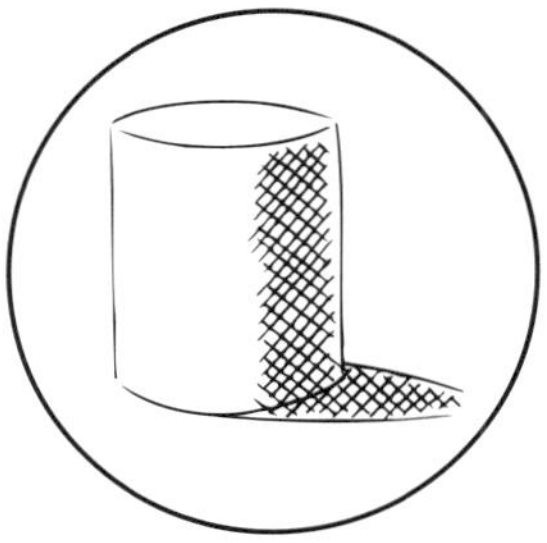

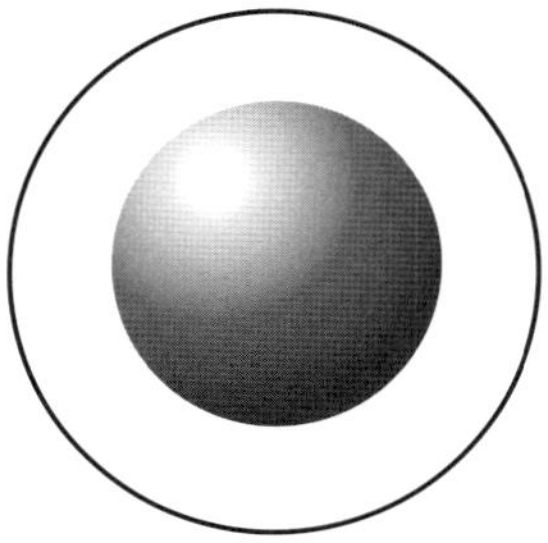

Name: Date:

Creating Depth with Shading

A. Look at the shading in each image. Draw arrows to show where light is coming from.

B. Find examples of shade or shading in magazines. Cut them out and glue them in the space below. Then highlight where the source of light is.

Pictures of Shading

Name: Date:

Creating Depth with Shading

Materials:

- 16 x 20" paper: white and black
- pencil, ruler, compass
- white chalk

Motivation:

To make a picture on black paper with all the basic shapes turned into forms by using white chalk to show where light reflects off the forms

What to Do:

1. On white paper, draw the outlines of the basic shapes of some still life objects with a pencil.

2. Then shade the dark sides of the objects to create the illusion of depth. These objects should appear to be forms (look three dimensional) because of the shading on one side. Important note: remember to use gradation in your shading.

3. Start on black paper and use the white chalk to draw and fill in the highlights (where light hits the object). These shapes will look like forms because areas of white chalk are used to show the lighted areas. It is important to remember to use gradation here, too.

Follow up:

Display the results for the enjoyment of all. Have students write a small explanation of what they think happened in this project and what they learned about shade from making these drawings.

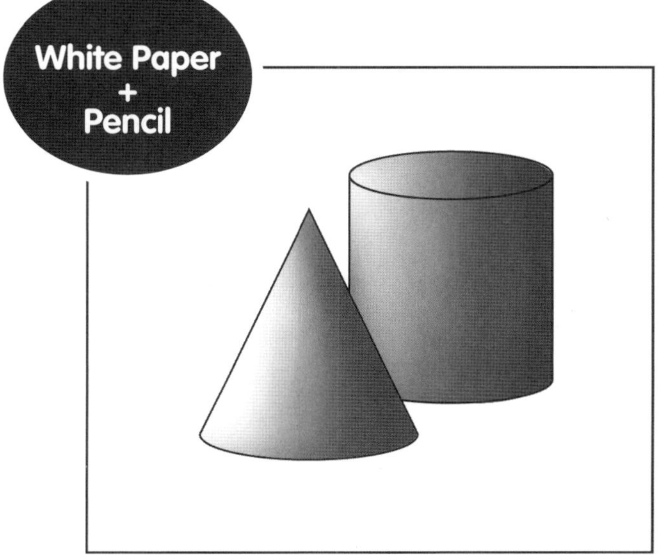

Name: Date:

Creating a Third Dimension with Shadows and Shading

Objective: *To demonstrate understanding that shadows and shading create the illusion of a third dimension*

We are going to add one more trick to creating the illusion of the third dimension in our art. It is something that has been following you for a long time – your shadow.

A **shadow** is the space that cannot be illuminated by direct light because of an obstruction. That obstruction could be anything, your body obstructing the sunlight from reaching the pavement, or a mail box obstructing the streetlight shining down on it. In each case, there would be a shaded area where the light source could not reach. Shadow is known as shade when it is transferred onto a two-dimensional picture, giving the illusion of a third dimension.

The process of filling in the shaded area of a shadow is known as shading. Examples of shaded forms in art, photography, on TV, and in magazines and newspapers are everywhere. Animated films took a leap forward in "looking real" when cartoons in moving images on screen were given shadows.

Shadows project the image or outline of the form that is obstructing the light source. There are many different varieties of light sources and they all affect how a shadow is cast differently. As a result, they also affect the techniques used to recreate the shaded areas in art.

Light sources can make shaded areas dark, light, short, or long. Lighting that is strong or close up creates darker shaded areas than lighting that is farther away or weak. If a light source is high above an object, the shadow will be short and closer to the object obstructing the light whereas if a light is low, the shadow will be long extending away from the obstruction. In order to recreate the correct depth of an object in a painting, drawing, or other work of art, you need to study the value of the shadow or shade of an object.

Name: Date:

Creating a Third Dimension with Shadows and Shading

Look at the shadow in each picture. Colour the correct circle yellow to indicate where the light source is. Then describe the light source as either "strong" or "weak" by circling the right word.

light source: strong / weak

light source: strong / weak

light source: strong / weak

light source: strong / weak

light source: strong / weak

light source: strong / weak

Name: Date:

Creating a Third Dimension with Shadows and Shading

A. Read each sentence and write either "true" or "false".

1. All types of lighting give the same type of shadow. ____________
2. Shading creates the illusion of a third dimension. ____________
3. Only large objects can obstruct light. ____________
4. Shadows cast the shape of the object obstructing the light source. ____________

B. Identify whether the image is missing either a shadow or shading. Then complete the image by adding the missing component.

1.

2.

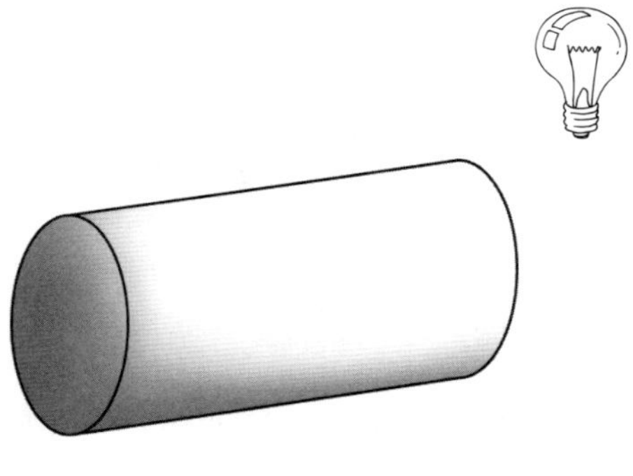

3.

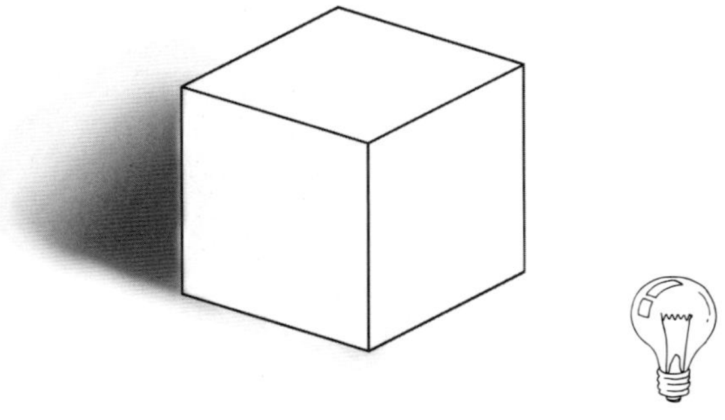

4.

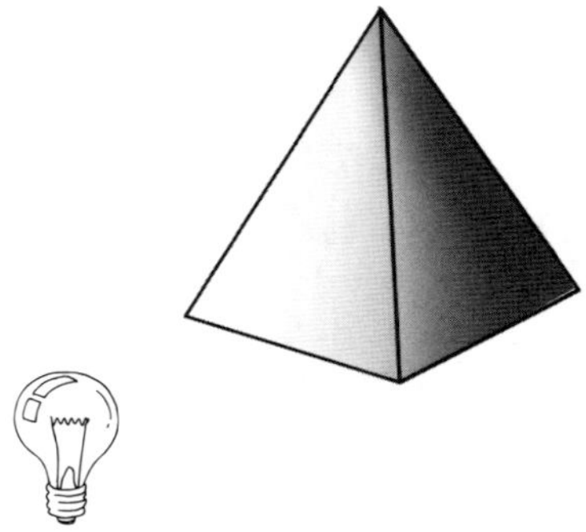

Name: Date:

Creating a Third Dimension with Shadows and Shading

Materials:

- 2 or 3 overhead projectors
- large sheet of black construction paper
- a pencil
- white paper or Bristol board
- masking tape
- a recent picture of yourself in profile
- glue
- scissors

Motivation:

To produce a two-dimensional piece of art that gives the illusion of a third dimension with the use of shadows and shading

What to Do:

1. Choose a partner to work with for the project.
2. Tape the piece of construction paper to the wall so that it is at the height of your partner's head.
3. Place the overhead projector in front of the wall so that it will illuminate the piece of paper.
4. Have your partner stand with either his or her left or right shoulder against the wall.
5. Line his or her head up with the piece of paper so that you will be able to trace his or her head's shadow onto the paper. Before you start tracing, make sure that the direction your partner is facing is the same as in the picture he or she has brought.
6. Turn on the overhead projector and trace the outline of the shadow with the pencil, making sure the entire shadow can fit on the page.
7. Repeat with the other partner.
8. Carefully cut out the profile and then glue it to the white paper or Bristol board.
9. Cut out your profile from the picture you brought in and glue it to the bottom of the page with your silhouette. It should look like a shadow of your head is being cast from your profile picture onto the page.

Art Lessons Grades 5-6

Drama and Dance

Name: Date:

Using Symbols and Props

Objective: *To identify the significance of symbols or props in drama, and use them appropriately*

It is said that a picture is worth a thousand words.

When telling your friend about a birthday present, you can use many different descriptive words. Your friend will try to imagine it, but he or she may not see it exactly as it is or the way you do. If you show your friend a picture of it, he or she will have no doubt about its appearance.

The art of "acting out" or **drama** has the same effect as showing someone a picture. Actors can show the audience something to make a lasting impression. Actors often use symbols or props to communicate their message more clearly.

A **symbol** is a visible sign or representation of an idea. A tear-stained letter might represent loss. An actor might use gestures, or arm movements, to symbolize grief or excitement. A **prop** is an object that one can move around as part of a production. This could be a telephone, clothes, furniture – any object that would help make the actor's message clearer.

Masks are one of the most common props used in drama. Their exaggerated facial features can both make the characters' emotions obvious and heighten the viewer's emotional responses to a dramatic piece. They can add a sense of humour or fear, depending on the mood of the play.

Masks originated from Greek drama, where one actor would play several different characters with the help of different masks. The audience could easily see who the villain, lover, or king was through the exaggerated expressions of the masks.

Today, masks are still used in Japanese Noh theatre. The main actor wears different masks to portray the many roles that he plays. Noh masks can be used to symbolize women, old men, and children, as well as different moods and personalities.

Name: Date:

Using Symbols and Props

Draw the emotion indicated on each of the masks below. Then colour them with appropriate colours to enhance their expressions.

Excitement

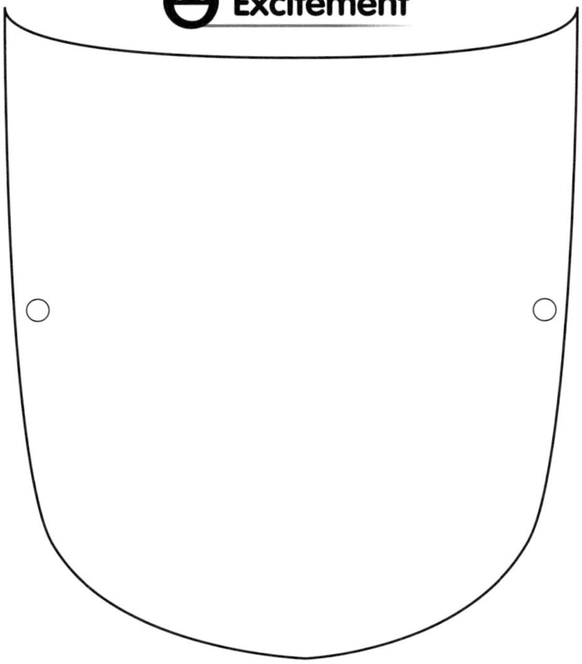

Sorrow

Fear

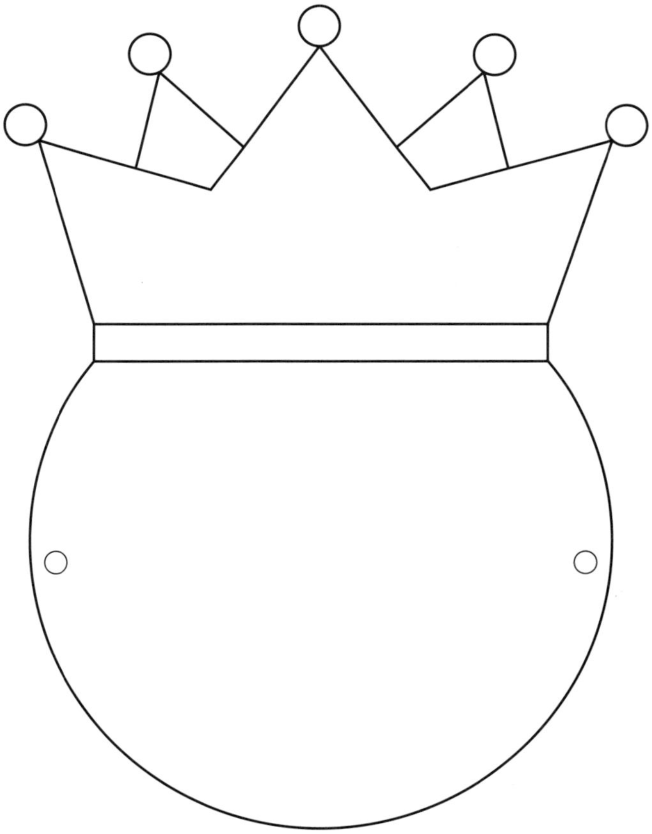

Name: Date:

Using Symbols and Props

Match the props to the correct characters. Cut them out and glue them to the appropriate characters.

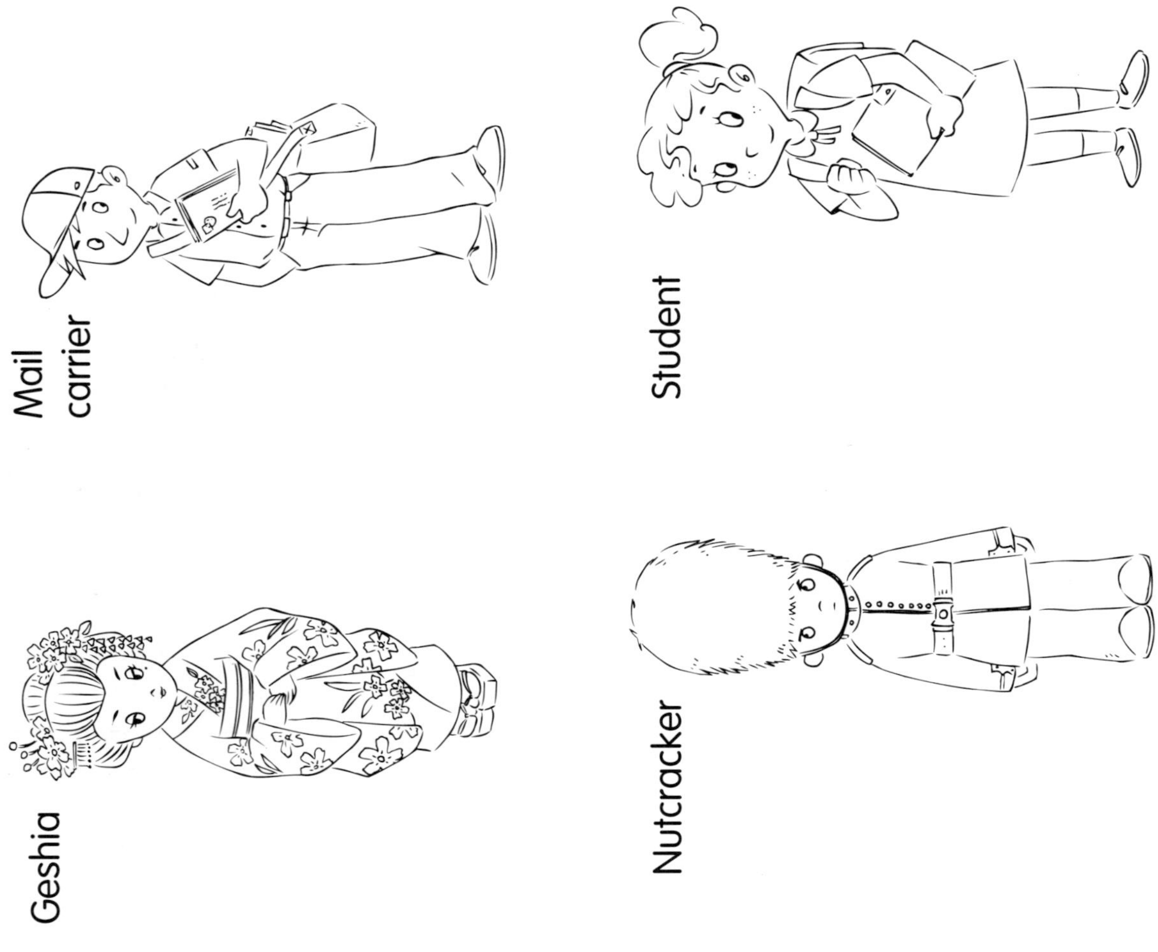

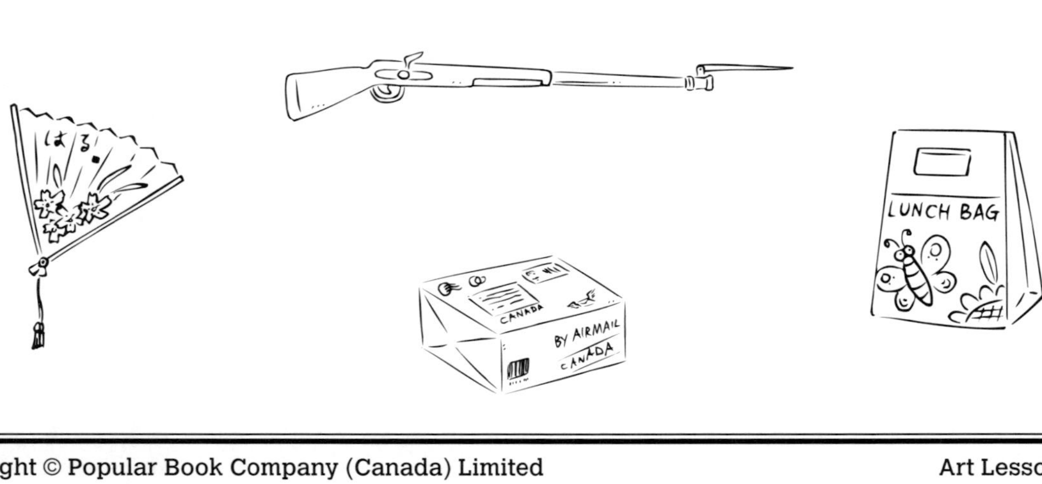

Name: Date:

Using Symbols and Props

Greek Theatre Masks

Materials:

- vaseline jelly
- plastic wrap
- plaster gauze – pre-cut into strips 2 – 4" long
- bowl with warm water and flour mixture (heavy, liquid consistency)
- large garbage bags or smocks
- paper towel
- acrylic paint, paintbrushes, mixing trays
- yarn, fur, and other decorations for fake hair
- Crayola Model Magic or other modelling clay

Motivation:

To explain the function of masks and their use in drama presentations

What to Do:

1 Sketch a mask on paper with coloured pencils, emphasizing the smile or frown, wrinkles, cheeks, and eyebrows. Use pictures of Greek masks or a friend as a model.

2 Find a partner. Cover his or her hair with plastic wrap. Apply Vaseline to his or her face, especially around the eyebrows, hair, and nose area so that the plaster won't stick to his or her face when it dries.

3 Dip the individual bandage strips into the water, gently remove excess mixture, and apply them to your partner's nose. Do not cover his or her air passageways – like the nostrils! Work out from there, covering all areas of the face (except around the eyes and mouth) to about 1 cm past the jaw line. Smooth away any rough bandage edges or bumps with your wet fingers.

4 Once your partner's face is covered, let it dry for about ten minutes. Then try to remove it by carefully lifting it off at the outer edges. Put it on a flat surface, as it continues to dry. Use plaster to smooth any roughness around the mouth or eye openings.

5 When the mask is completely dry, sand it with sandpaper. Use pieces of Model Magic to create wrinkles, sags, bags, cheeks, and chins.

6 Apply a base coat of Gesso, varnish, or white glue and water to keep the paint from soaking into the plaster.

7 Form a "wig" with the yarn or fur by gluing it to the top part of the mask. Then use paint to decorate the mask and to bring out the expressions.

Name: Date:

Performing in Public

Objective: *To describe skills needed to perform in public*

Imagine you are in front of your class doing a presentation, and a sea of eyes are looking right at you. Your throat becomes dry, you feel faint, and when you speak, only a squeak comes out.

Nervousness, we all experience it. How is it overcome? First, we must start by knowing our material. If we are prepared, we will find it much easier to perform in public.

In addition, there are several skills you can work on to make your performance top notch:

1. **VOICE:**

   Practise speaking loudly. Use your voice to project to the very back of the room. Make a word or line stand out by whispering or yelling it. Use pauses to give the audience a moment to digest what you have said. Pronounce your words clearly and use expression!

2. **EYE CONTACT:**

   Include all of the audience, looking at their eyes...or foreheads. Pick someone whom you feel comfortable with to keep looking back to. If you are speaking for a longer period, pretend there are X's on the side and back walls, moving your eyes between them. Try to avoid focusing on the roof or floor.

3. **GESTURES:**

   Use variety but be selective, keeping your hands above your waist and off your hair, face, and clothes. Try using your hands to show these types of gestures:

   a. emphatic – "This is up to YOU!"
   b. prompting – "Let's hear it for..."
   c. descriptive – to clarify, create image, define measurement
   d. suggestive – present thought, idea, or emotion

Lastly, use your body to get into the role you are playing. How would the character's face look in a particular situation? How would he or she move across the stage? It's your chance to be someone else for a bit – so have fun!

Name: Date:

Performing in Public

Answer the questions. Then try out your answers with your friends.

Voice: What kind of voice would you use to say these lines?

1. "Get out!" ____________________

2. "Please, don't go." ____________________

3. "Good morning, Sweetie." ____________________

Eye Contact: Where would you look while performing these pieces publicly?

1. A dialogue with another character ____________________

2. A class presentation ____________________

Gestures: What gestures would accompany these events?

1. Accusing someone of something ____________________

2. Greeting someone in an office ____________________

3. Inviting someone to have a seat ____________________

Name: Date:

Performing in Public

Find as many pictures as you can in magazines illustrating the actions or gestures below. Then cut them out and glue them in the space provided. Check off the actions and gestures you have found.

Showing Different Expressions

- ○ glaring angrily
- ○ yelling
- ○ "No!" (gesture)
- ○ looking hopelessly
- ○ whispering
- ○ "My pleasure!" (gesture)
- ○ staring astonishingly

Practise some of these expressions in the mirror!

Name: Date:

Performing in Public

Readers' Theatre

Materials:

- *The Gifts of Wali Dad: A Tale of India and Pakistan*
- *The Baker's Dozen: A Saint Nicholas Tale*

Motivation:

To interpret and communicate the meaning of novels, scripts, legends, fables, and other material drawn from a range of sources and cultures, using a variety of drama techniques

What to Do:

1. In groups, decide who will be playing each role.
2. Consider the voice and facial expressions that each character would have.
3. Practise reading the script a few times. Remember to speak clearly and project your voices. Use expression to bring the script to life.
4. Learn each of your lines so that you can look up from your script when it is your turn. Use your hands to emphasize words or phrases.
5. Present your Readers' Theatre to the class.
6. One person reads the story while the others act out the events and speak their lines.

Follow up:

How did the authors use the plot to share a moral? Can you relate to any of the main characters in these stories? Which presentation did you like best? Why?

Name: Date:

In Character

Objective: *To create characters and portray their motives and decisions through speech and movement*

We appreciate the work of famous actors and actresses because it makes us laugh, cry, or feel other emotions. Their performances not only move us but also teach us more about people through the characters they play in film, television, or theatre. There are many different kinds of characters, just like there are many different kinds of people in real life.

Characters in a story could be:

honest, light-hearted, brave, conceited, mischievous, demanding, thoughtful, keen, happy, disagreeable, creative, intelligent, gentle, proud, messy, energetic...

How would you act out these character traits in front of an audience? How would you show a motive or a choice through the way a character speaks or moves?

It is important to consider the questions above carefully, but it is even more important not to change your actions or train of thought once you have decided how you will represent your character. It is important to stay "in character", otherwise your character will not be convincing! When a performer stops acting like the character he or she is attempting to portray, he or she is said to be "breaking character". So remember, think of what the character you are playing would do, say, or how he or she would act to get into that character.

Name:

Date:

In Character

Get into the following characters. Write how they would speak and describe their emotions and movements.

The Tortoise And The Hare

voice: ______________ ______________

emotion: ______________ ______________

movements: ______________ ______________

Three Blind Mice

voice: ______________

____

emotion: ______________

____

movements: ______________

____

Goldilocks and the Three Bears

voice: ______________ ______________

emotion: ______________ ______________

movements: ______________ ______________

Name: Date:

In Character

A. Read the events below and write whether the performers are "in character" or if they are "breaking character" on the given lines.

1. A scared little girl in a dark scary place starts to giggle. ____________________
2. The actress playing "Sister Bear" continues her performance even though her costume rips. ____________________
3. A boy playing the role of "The King" forgets his lines and starts crying during a monologue. ____________________
4. An actor continues using his adopted accent even though the play is over. ____________________

B. Look at the picture and write what the boy's character would be saying if he were "in character".

____

____

____

Name: Date:

In Character

What Really Happened...

Materials:

- variety of costume materials, colourful cloth, etc.
- materials for props (cardboard, markers, actual props)

Motivation:

To create, rehearse, and present dramatic works to communicate the meaning of poems, stories, paintings, myths, and other source materials

What to Do:

1. Choose a well-known fairy tale or children's story. These could include *The Three Little Bears*, *Little Red Riding Hood*, *The Three Billy Goats Gruff*, *The Three Little Pigs*, etc.
2. Think of what all these stories have in common. Is there always a hero/heroine? Is good versus evil? Is there a moral to the story?
3. In groups, rewrite one of the stories from a different point of view. You are going to show the audience what really happened. Maybe Little Red Riding Hood is actually very demanding, or maybe Goldilocks is forgetful. Perhaps the big, bad wolf is a scaredy pants after all. All the characters and settings should be the same, but the storyline needs to be altered.
4. Change the personalities and use the element of suspense to tell your story. Modernize it. Make it entertaining.
5. Write out the lines or a basic outline of the happenings and feel free to improvise (make up your own words while you are acting out your character).
6. Create costumes and props from provided materials. Practise acting out your story, paying attention to how your character speaks and moves.
7. Present your dramatic piece to the class.

Name: Date:

Marvellous Movement

Objective: *To describe various dance forms*

Scottish country dance

What do you feel like doing when you hear great music? Maybe your foot stomps the ground a little, or you tap the table with your fingers. Does your whole body want to join in?

Since the beginning of mankind, people have used movement creatively. It is a way to express ideas and feelings that are important in people's daily lives.

Dancers can be trained in various kinds of dance; ballet, jazz, hip hop, and tap are only a few of today's most popular styles. Many appreciate watching dances on stage or performing them socially with friends and family at weddings or other celebrations.

Movement is often used as a form of self-expression that can represent your feelings or experiences. How do you move when you hear your favourite song? Dance movements vary between individuals but are also unique across cultures and historical periods. Did you know that "Cha-cha-cha" is the name of a Latin-American dance, like the Rumba and Samba? These Latin dances are fast paced and energetic. If you slow the music down, you might get the right tempo for a Waltz or a slow Foxtrot.

Folk dances are traditional cultural dances with precise and organized movements. Some popular folk dances include: Irish dance, which has rapid and detailed leg and foot movements, but holds a rigid upper body; Nordic polska dance, which involves a series of little half steps; Israeli folk dance that can involve a circle formation including large groups of dancers; and Scottish highland dancing, where dancers use the balls of their feet to perform very impressive footwork! The movements of these and other traditional, cultural dances are all quite different. Some are slow, dragging movements and others are quick. What movements do you like to use when you dance?

Western square dance

Name: Date:

Marvellous Movement

Pretend you are creating a dance to celebrate the seasons. For each, write five movements you would use to signify the season you are celebrating.

Spring

Summer

Fall

Winter

Summer

My movements for summer will be quick and busy-like!

Name: Date:

Marvellous Movement

Create your own interpretive dance. Think of an event, an argument, a celebration, or a story. Break the event up into three parts: introduction, conflict, and conclusion. For each part, provide four to six movements that illustrate or "tell" the event. Then perform your dance for an audience.

Part I Introduction: __________

Movements: __________

Part II Conflict: __________

Movements: __________

Part III Conclusion: __________

Movements: __________

Name: Date:

Marvellous Movement

Dance Sequence

Materials:

- None!

Motivation:

To demonstrate the use of different patterns in creating different effects in dance

What to Do:

1. Have the teacher start by creating a sequence of three or four uncomplicated movements.
2. Then have the class repeat these movements.
3. One by one each student will add his or her own movement to the teacher's initial sequence.

Follow up:

Reflect on the routine your class has created and try to find a piece of music that is harmonious with it, and reflects its movements and style.

Name: Date:

Reaching the Audience

Objective: *To explain how elements of drama and dance can have different effects on the audience*

Have you ever laughed out loud while watching TV? Or has a sad show ever made you cry?

Entertainers use different elements and techniques to move their audience:

They make the **characters** believable so that you can relate to them. They want you to be able to feel their emotions and understand their decisions. They want you to feel like you are a part of a performance's conflict or resolution. The **structure** (or storyline) of the drama is designed to hold your interest by addressing real life events. Scenes change quickly so that you do not get bored, and turn your attention to something else.

The element of **suspense** is used to keep you on the edge of your seat. It is often created with music and lighting. These effects are used to reach the audience by stimulating many senses at once, making their experience more intense.

In dance, the **timing** of music and movement is very important. The **energy** of a dance is also contagious and can invite the audience to join in. Upbeat music calls the audience to smile and clap along. Lighting can add to the mood created by the dancers' movements. The dancers themselves reach the audience through their facial expressions. By reading the emotions on the dancers' faces, the audience is able to understand the overall mood of the dance piece.

Performance artists have an incredible ability to influence their audience. The use of music, lighting, staging, and other effects seem only to enrich the performances they give. Together, these elements are able to change a viewer's mood, opinion, or response!

Name: Date:

Reaching the Audience

For each performance, give three factors that could be used to reach the audience.

A Clown Show

A Ballet

An Action Movie

A Dramatic Play

Factors Used to Reach the Audience

A Clown Show

____

____

____

A Ballet

____

____

____

An Action Movie

____

____

____

A Dramatic Play

____

____

____

Name: Date:

Reaching the Audience

Think of a time when you felt scared, excited, happy, or sad because of a performance you saw. Then fill in the information and draw a scene illustrating the moment in the performance that affected you the most.

Performance Title: ______________________________

Emotion Felt: ______________________________

Factors Causing the Emotion: ______________________________

____

____

Impressive Scene

Name: Date:

Reaching the Audience

Shadow Puppets

Materials:

- short stories to use as a framework
- black Bristol board
- wooden shish-kabob skewers
- paper fasteners
- thin, vinyl shower curtain
- spot lamp and various coloured cellophane (used as a filter)

Motivation:

To produce a short script that makes use of a variety of techniques to create different effects for different audiences

Shadow shows are an ancient art. They were used in China's Song Dynasty and were popular across the social classes. Because facial expressions and body movements are limited, the music, sounds, and lighting are very important in telling a story using shadows.

What to Do:

In groups, create a simple, short script retelling a short story.

1. Set up a shadow puppet theatre. Drape an inexpensive white shower curtain so there is room between it and the light source for the puppeteers to work.

2. Decide which characters you will include. Outline your puppet on the Bristol board and cut it out. Remember that your puppet will be viewed from the side.

3. If you are making a moving puppet, make sure you allow enough overlap on moving pieces (e.g. arms). Use a paper fastener to attach the two pieces.

4. Attach one skewer perpendicularly to the main puppet part and another to the part that moves, if applicable.

5. Turn off all other lights, and practise using the puppets with the light source from behind, revealing the image or "shadow" on the screen or wall. Prepare the music and lighting and start your performance.

Follow up:

Would the play be as effective without the lighting and music?

Name: Date:

Drama and Dance in the Community

Objective: *To identify the function of dance and drama in the community and their contributions to the economy*

Have you ever participated in a school play, or been to a local film festival?

The arts create many jobs; from advertising to electrical work, there is a need for almost every trade out there! Carpenters are used to build the sets, and costumes depend on the skill of dressmakers and clothing manufacturers. The people selling tickets at the box office have a role too. Most of these workers can be found within your community. Drama and dance performances can almost be seen as one big community project!

Some cities depend a lot on the entertainment industry. Larger cities such as Toronto and Vancouver have an active theatre district, where you can watch anything from musicals or ballet, to murder mystery dinner theatre. Local performing arts bring together our national community, and provide quality experiences for people all over the country.

Smaller cities are involved in the performing arts, too. Stratford, Ontario, has visitors come from all over the world to see performances of Shakespearean plays.

The performing arts should be valued and supported in our communities; they entertain us, bring us together, educate us, and can give us a different perspective on our world.

Name: Date:

Drama and Dance in the Community

Find a brochure or advertisement for a performance that took place or will take place in your community. Cut it out and glue it in the space below. Then answer the questions.

A Performance in My Community

1. Give four benefits of including the performing arts in your community.

2. Name three occupations involved in producing a community play and the services they lend to the dramatic piece.

Occupations	**Services Provided**

Name: Date:

Drama and Dance in the Community

Plan a performing arts piece for your community. Then present your idea to the class.

Think of something that will educate and include members of your community.

A Performing Arts Piece for My Community

- Kind of Piece: ____________________
  e.g. play, dance, musical, etc.
- Target Audience: children / teenagers / adults / families
- What It Will Be about:
  ____
  ____
  ____
  ____
- Location: ____________________
- Number of Performers: __________
- Who Will Play What:
  ____
  ____
  ____
  ____

Name: Date:

Drama and Dance in the Community

Advertising the Arts

Materials:

- markers, pencil crayons
- Bristol board
- pictures

Motivation:

To make a poster to highlight/advertise the local performance

Commercials are used to advertise the arts. After researching a current performance, think of how you will get more people out to see it!

What to Do:

1. Look on the Internet or in brochures found in your community to find out the current performances in your area. Choose one you would like to support.

2. Learn as much as you can about this production. What is the style? What kind of music will be played? What audience is targeted? (Is it for kids, elderly, adults, or a mix of age groups?)

3. How will you get others to be interested in this performance?

4. Make a poster to advertise the event.

Checklists

Name: Date:

Checklist: Music

- [ ] I can recognize, interpret, and read familiar and unfamiliar whole notes, half-notes, quarter notes, and eighth-notes, and the corresponding rests in 4/4 time.
- [ ] I can conduct in 4/4 time and 2/4 time, using standard conducting patterns.
- [ ] I can recognize the major scale through listening and in notation.
- [ ] I understand the meaning of sharp, flat, and natural symbols.
- [ ] I am able to sing or play the major scale in keys that occur in the music I sing or play.
- [ ] I can identify the form of introduction, verse, and chorus in music that I sing, play, or hear.
- [ ] I recognize different kinds of tone colour in pieces of music.
- [ ] I recognize and can classify various instruments.
- [ ] I can sing and play in tune.
- [ ] I can identify simple structural patterns in music that I sing, play, or hear.
- [ ] I can identify music that consists of a single line as monophonic.

Name: Date:

Checklist: Visual Arts

- ☐ I can identify three pairs of complementary colours.
- ☐ I can identify colour relationships using a basic colour wheel.
- ☐ I can describe how lines can be used to define shapes and forms, and to create movement.
- ☐ I understand that lines can be used to direct the viewer's attention.
- ☐ I understand that shading can be used to create the illusion of depth (a third dimension).
- ☐ I can identify negative and positive shapes in works of art and in the environment.
- ☐ I understand the relationship between a work of art and its surroundings.
- ☐ I can identify tools and techniques used by artists to create the illusion of texture.
- ☐ I can describe the strengths and limitations of various art tools, materials, and techniques.
- ☐ I am able to select the most appropriate tools, materials, and techniques for a particular purpose, and use them correctly.
- ☐ I know the things to be considered when placing a sculpture in a specific location.
- ☐ I can describe how artists use texture to represent or evoke an emotional response.

Name: Date:

Checklist: Drama and Dance

- ☐ I demonstrate awareness of audience when writing in role.
- ☐ I use and sustain appropriate language, tone of voice, gestures, and body movements when speaking as a character in a drama.
- ☐ I can use drama vocabulary when describing and interpreting my own and others' work.
- ☐ I can explain drama and dance techniques and use them to convey information and feelings.
- ☐ I can identify the significance of symbols and objects in drama and dance, and use props appropriately.
- ☐ I am able to sustain concentration in drama and dance.
- ☐ I understand the use of technology in creating contrasting effects.
- ☐ I can describe various dance forms.
- ☐ I can describe the skills needed to perform in public.

Art Lessons Grades 5-6

Project Ideas

Name: Date:

Pointillism

Materials:

- blank white paper
- eraser
- cotton swabs
- sharp thin pencil
- tempera paint

Create an image using pointillism style painting to gain an understanding of the strengths and weaknesses of this particular artistic technique.

What to Do:

1. Take the blank white paper and put it on top of the flamingo image on page 149.
2. With your pencil, lightly trace the image on page 149 onto the blank page.
3. Take the cotton swab and dip it in the paint. Then fill each of the sections in the image by making individual dots side by side. Do not let the paint merge together. Keep all the dots separate. Paint each section using only the colour indicated; otherwise you will not be able to make out the inner details of the image.
4. When you are finished, let your work dry.
5. When dry, gently erase the pencil marks.

Compare your work to that of Georges Seurat. Does your image also appear dream like?

La Parade
George Seurat

Name: Date:

Pointillism

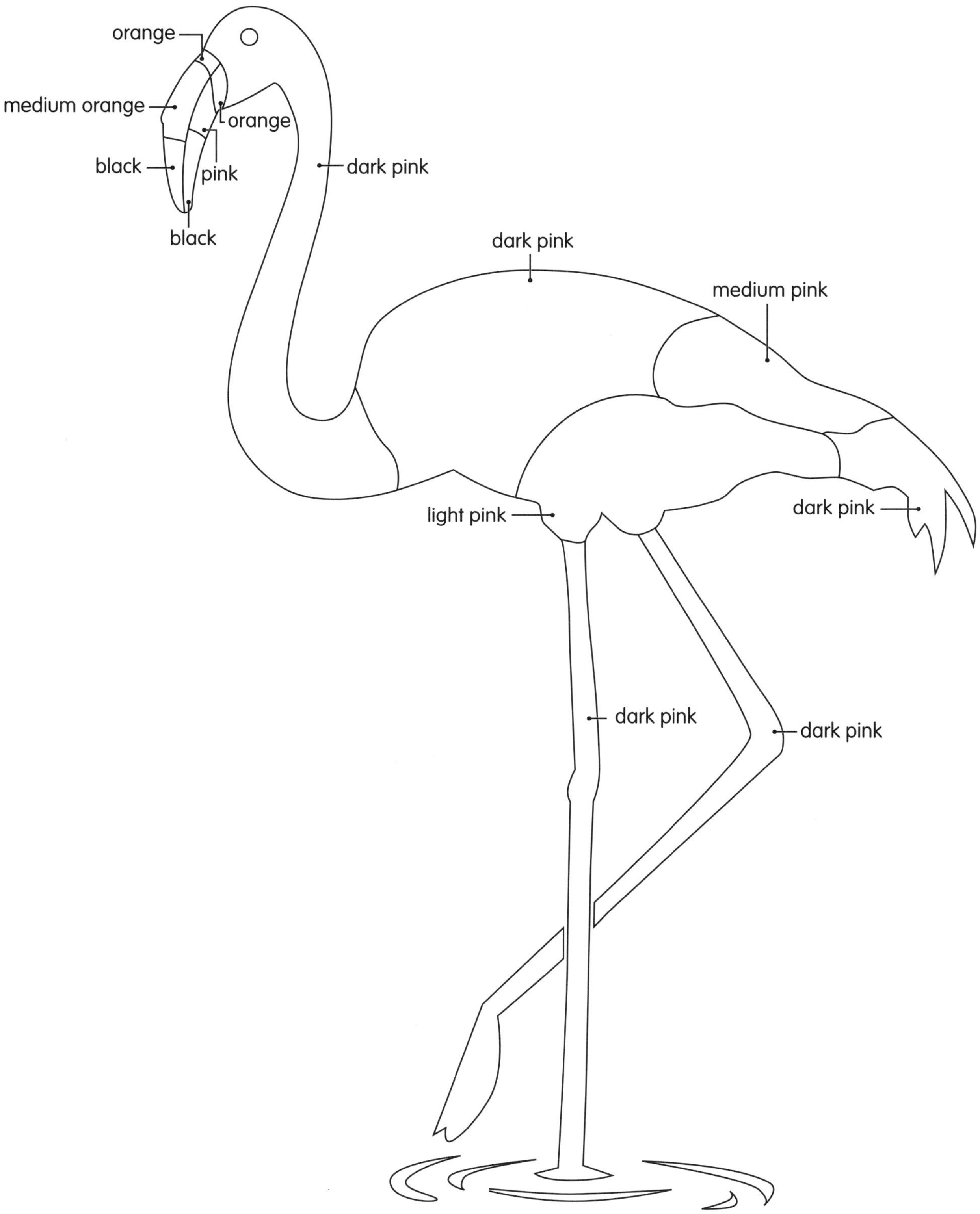

Name: Date:

Drawing What You Really See

What you draw may not always be what you see and what you see isn't always what you draw.

Materials:

- pencils
- paper
- large object

What to Do:

1 The teacher should display a large object for the students to draw, in front of the class. Make sure they can all see the object.

2 Have the students take their pencil and paper and begin drawing the outline of the object together. Make sure they take their time and that they do not look down at their page. They must keep their eyes on the object at all times!

3 Their eyes and pencil should be synchronized as they draw the outline. They should draw the entire outline of the object without lifting their pencil.

4 Once they've finished the outline, tell them to add the rest of the details to their drawing one by one – without looking at their hand as it is drawing!

5 When finished, have them look at their drawing and observe the differences between what their eyes saw and what their hand registered on the page.

6 Answer the following questions:

- Which parts of the drawing look similar to the object and which are completely different?
- What should they have done differently?
- Why do their drawings look different from the actual object?

Display all of the students' drawings in a line, starting with the drawing that looks closest to the object and finishing with the one that looks least like the object. Do not display the children's names on the drawings.

Vase with flowers

Name: Date:

Just Like Picasso

Materials:

- 4 pieces of paper
- pencil
- pencil crayons

What to Do:

Using the Internet or library, find and study the following portraits by Picasso:

- *Portrait de Jacqueline de Face.II* – 1962
- *Seated Woman with Wrist Watch* – 1932
- *Portrait of Dora Maar* – 1937

1 Work in pairs.

2 Study your partner from all angles (consider the shape of his or her face, the depth of the lines in his or her face or eyes, the texture of his or her hair or skin, etc.)

3 Draw the outline of your partner's face from the front and sides (both left and right) using a black marker on three different pieces of paper. Make sure to make the outlines the same size – about the length and width of the page.

4 Take each drawing starting with the front perspective and trace them one on top of the other onto the fourth, blank page.

5 Switch and repeat the activity.

6 Compare your work with that of Picasso's.

Landscapes, Fauve Style

Materials:

- paintbrush
- colouring crayons or paint
- 2 copies of the landscape image provided

What to Do:

1. Use strong colours and unrealistic values to colour or paint one of the landscape images provided.
2. Use natural colours and values to paint or colour the other.
3. When they are done, compare them to see which you prefer.

Fauve Style

Artists who painted in the Fauve style used bold and unrealistic colours to paint everyday objects. Although this movement did not last long, the mark it made on the art world was significant.

Woman with a Hat
Henri Matisse, 1905

Name: Date:

Landscapes, Fauve Style

Name: Date:

Crazy Surrealist Collage

Create a surprising and unexpected figure similar to those made by popular surrealist artists!

Materials:

- old magazines
- scissors
- glue
- construction paper
- pencils (one per student)
- long strips of paper (one per student)

What to Do:

1. Fold the long strips of paper into 6 sections.

2. Open the long strip of paper.

3. Write (1) on the first section. Fold the section to hide it. Pass it to the classmate next to you – you should receive one in return. Write (2) on the next section. Fold the section to hide it. Pass it to the classmate next to you – you should receive one in return. Repeat until (1) to (6) have been completed.

4. Open the paper you are left with and read the sequence. It should read as follows:

(1)	(2)	(3)	(4)	(5)	(6)
an article and an adjective	a noun	a verb (past tense)	a preposition	an article and an adjective	a noun

5. Use the sequence of words on the long piece of paper as a guideline to creating a collage of a creature out of magazine pictures.

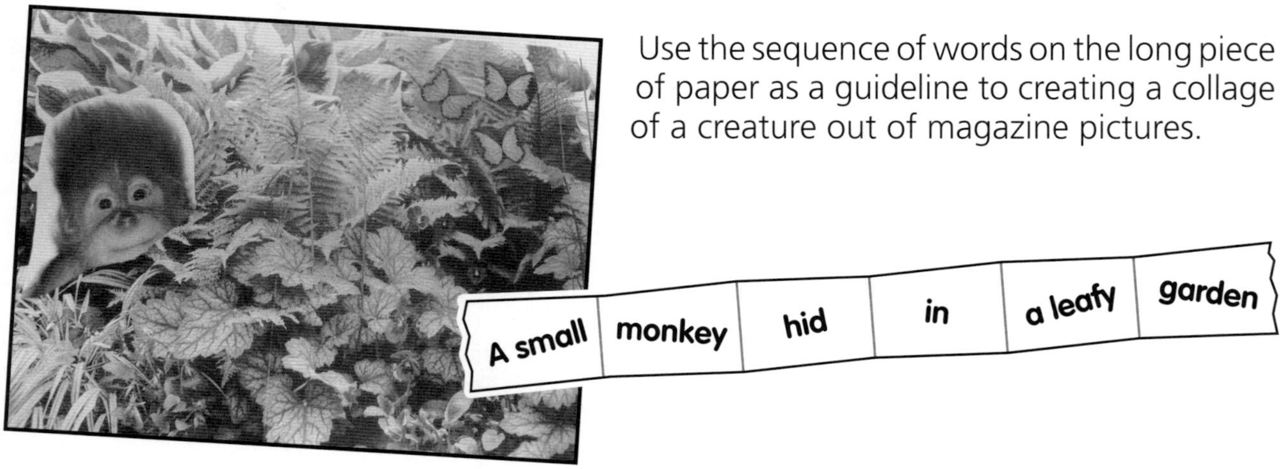

Name: Date:

Foil Painting

Create texture and movement like Van Gogh, and gain knowledge of the strengths and limitations of aluminum foil as an art material!

Materials:

- 8.5 x 11″ cardboard
- 9.5 x 12″ aluminum foil (heavy duty)
- black permanent marker
- blank white paper
- tempera paint
- paintbrushes
- tape

What to Do:

1. Cover one side of the cardboard with the aluminum foil by wrapping it like a present and taping it in place. Make sure the shiny side faces out.
2. Draw an image on the white piece of paper. It could be anything: a pattern, an object, an animal, or even a person. Make sure the drawing is elaborate and covers most of the paper.
3. Hold the paper with your drawing over the aluminum foil.
4. With a dull pencil, trace the drawing. Press down hard enough to engrave the drawing into the foil.
5. Once you have finished, remove the paper and trace the transferred design on the foil using the black permanent marker.
6. Then paint the drawing on the aluminum foil using the tempera paint and a dry paintbrush.

Find a partner. Take a look at both of your works. Then discuss the strengths and limitations of aluminum foil as an art material. Write a summary for your teacher.

Name: Date:

My Favourite Musical Instrument

Materials:

- Bristol board
- glue
- scissors

Share your favourite musical instrument with your class by making an informative presentation!

The Guitar

How do you play it?

You hold it across your body diagonally, so that your left hand can hold the strings on the fingerboard and your right hand can pluck the strings, or strum them with a pick.

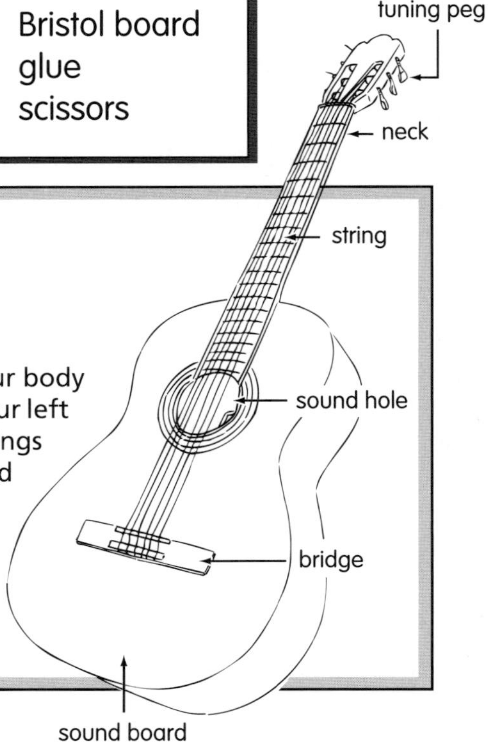

What to Do:

1 Choose an instrument to write about. (Make sure everyone in the class has chosen a different instrument.)

2 Find pictures of this instrument.

3 Find variations of your favourite instrument that exist in different cultures or countries (if there are any). Get pictures of them as well.

4 Answer the following questions:

- What are the components of the instrument? (label a picture)
- How does it make sound? (draw a diagram)
- What kind of sound does it make? (describe pitch)
- What kind of music uses this type of sound? (give audio examples)
- What material can it be or what is it usually made of? (Does its material affect the sound?)
- When was it invented?
- Who is famous for playing your favourite instrument?

5 Compile all of your information into a display on Bristol board and present it to the class.

Name: Date:

Dance Movement Freeze

Materials:

- 5 to 10 different music varieties of various tempos
- music player
- timer

Use dance techniques to convey information and feelings. Demonstrate your ability to sustain concentration in dance!

What to Do:

1. Choose one person to be the guesser.
2. The guesser is given a timer and should be escorted somewhere where they will not be able to hear the music.
3. Once the guesser is out of ear shot, they should start the timer. The teacher should then start the music and the other students should start dancing. The dancers must make movements that reflect the music being played.
4. After 15 to 30 seconds, the teacher stops the music and the dancers "freeze" in their positions/movements.
5. The guesser must then enter the room and try to guess the style of music that was playing based on the students' body positions (rock&roll, classical, etc.).
6. Once the music style has been guessed, switch the guesser and the music and try again!

Name: Date:

Make a Rain Stick!

Create a musical instrument, and experience the sounds and ways it can make music!

Materials:

- paper towel tube
- scissors
- masking tape
- construction paper
- popcorn kernels
- markers
- 2 aluminum foil pieces (6" wide, 1.5 times the length of the tube)

What to Do:

1. Take the aluminum foil pieces and crumple them, keeping their length.
2. Twist the long snake-like aluminum foil pieces into 2 coils and put them aside.
3. Fold the construction paper in half, bringing the two shortest ends together.
4. Draw a large circle on each side of the folded line and cut out the circles.
5. Make two circles, by tracing the end of the tube, in the middle of each larger circle.
6. Draw 9 evenly spaced lines from the outline of the larger circle to the outline of the smaller tube-sized circle. Cut along these lines to create spokes.
7. Put both aluminum coils into the tube.
8. Cover one end of the tube with the construction paper and fold the spokes to form a cap over the end of the tube. Then tape them in place.
9. Put the popcorn kernels into the tube and repeat step 8, covering the other end of the tube.
10. Decorate your tube with markers. Then tip it up and down to hear the sound your rain stick makes!

Name: Date:

Make a Rain Stick!

Work with a partner to write a poem that can be enriched by the sound of your rain stick. Then perform it in front of your class!

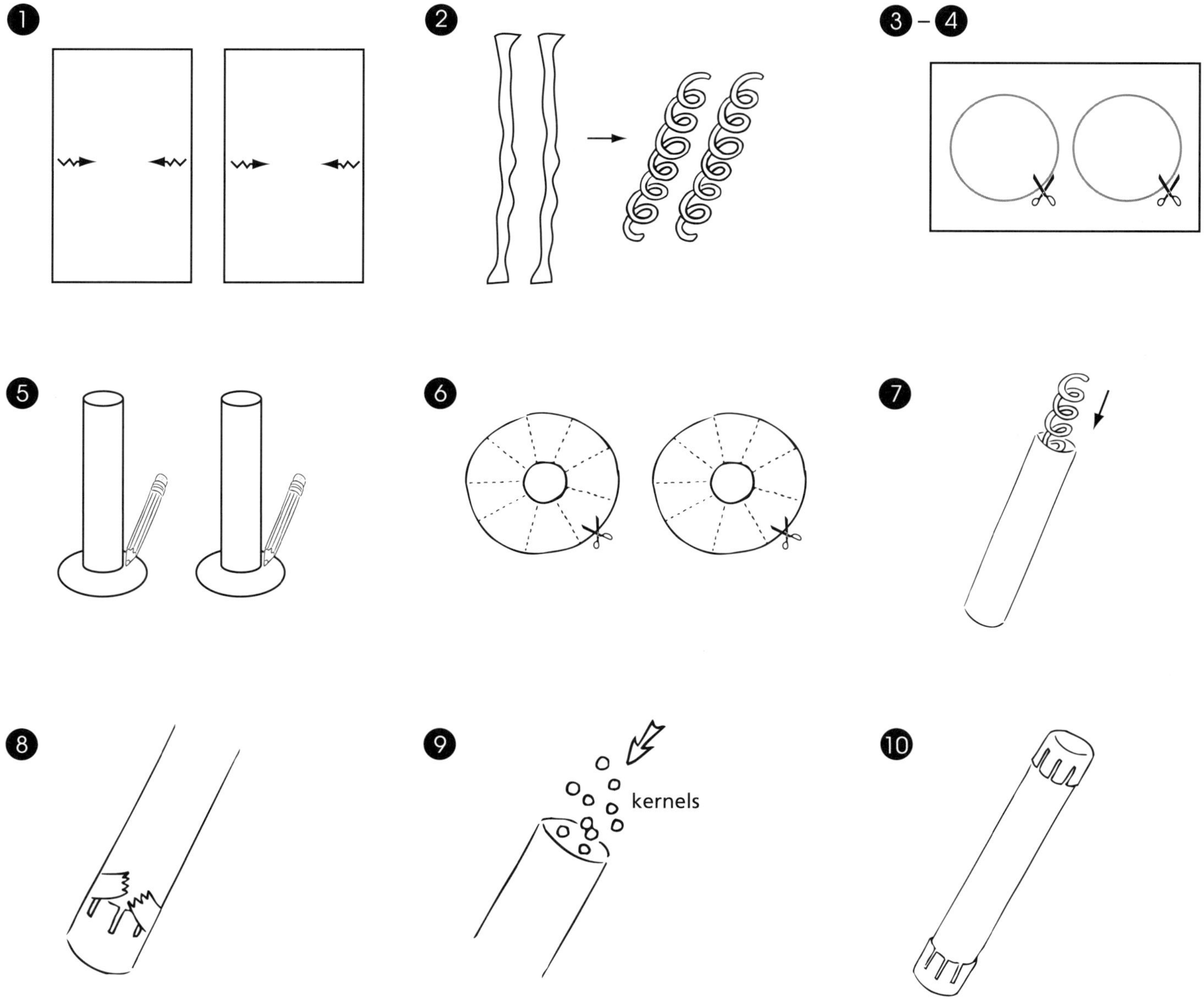

Name that Invention!

Spot the significance and appropriate uses of symbols and props in dramatic explorations!

Materials:

- paper
- pencils
- box

What to Do:

1. Have everyone in the class write down a famous invention and put it in the box.

2. Divide the class into three or four groups. There should be around six or more people per group.

3. Have each group pick one invention out of the box without looking.

4. Then allow the groups a few minutes to read the invention they have picked, and plan a short skit that they will present in front of the other groups. Have one person write down each symbol or prop that will be used. The objective is to try and get the other groups to guess the famous invention.

5. Each observing group will write down their guess and submit it to the teacher after the skit is done as well as a list of props/symbols that they saw used.

6. The group that guesses the invention correctly gets a point and acts out their silent skit/ play next.

7. Additional points are given for each correct symbol/prop written down by the group. (one point for guessing the invention and an additional point for every correct prop/symbol mentioned)

8. Continue this game until all inventions in the box have been guessed.

Results of Naming the Invention

Game / Group								Total